THE GOVERNMENT AND POLITICS OF CALIFORNIA

THE GOVERNMENT
AND POLITICS
OF
FOURTH EDITION
CALIFORNIA

HENRY A. TURNER
University of California, Santa Barbara

JOHN A. VIEG
California State Polytechnic College, Pomona

McGRAW-HILL BOOK COMPANY

New York   San Francisco   St. Louis   Düsseldorf   Johannesburg
Kuala Lumpur   London   Mexico   Montreal   New Delhi   Panama
Rio de Janeiro   Singapore   Sydney   Toronto

This book was set in Electra by Monotype Composition Company, and printed on permanent paper and bound by Peninsula Lithograph Company. The designer was Janet Bollow; the drawings were done by Judith McCarty. The editors were Robert P. Rainier and Michael A. Ungersma. Charles A. Goehring supervised production.

THE GOVERNMENT AND POLITICS OF CALIFORNIA

Printed in the United States of America.

Library of Congress catalog card number: 72–144770

4567890   EBEB   098765

The publication of the fourth edition of *The Government and Politics of California* coincides with the beginning of a new political era in California. The 1970 census officially established California as the most populous state; it now has the largest delegation in Congress and at national political party conventions, and the largest electoral vote. Thus its already substantial influence in national affairs will in all probability increase. Other changes have occurred on the state's political scene. A variety of problems—for example, racial inequality, traffic congestion, air pollution, juvenile delinquency, and crime—have assumed greater proportions than formerly, and their solutions require new approaches and greatly expanded efforts. Many Californians have apparently endorsed new and different political attitudes and forms of political activity, as is indicated by protest movements and street and campus demonstrations. Noteworthy, too, are the widespread insistence that greater consideration be given to the quality of life and the tendency to question the traditional value placed on bigness and growth. In brief, various developments have led us to believe that California politics in the 1970s will be considerably different from the 1960s and that, in order to meet the needs of this new era, *The Government and Politics of California* should be essentially a new book. The central focus of this edition is on the pervasive influence of politics on every phase of California state and local government.

To make the book more suitable for use with supplementary readings we have reduced the number of chapters from twelve to eight and have shortened the contents by approximately one-third. The reduction has been achieved primarily by reorganizing and condensing certain sections, excluding topics customarily covered by national government books, and eliminating much of the historical data and descriptions of administrative agencies. Although shorter, the book presents a comprehensive coverage of all significant aspects of California government and politics, including the state constitution, direct democracy, and the powers, functions, and organization of the legislative, executive, and judicial branches of the government. Two full chapters are devoted to political parties, political interest groups, elections, political campaigns, and related topics. Attention is called to critical problems confronting the state, and to needed governmental reform. Throughout all eight chapters the emphasis is on political dynamics. In addition to being reorganized, revised, and rewritten, the book has been completely updated throughout. The 1970 election and all other important political events and developments occuring in California since the publication of the third edition have been analyzed and discussed. We have attempted through improvements in style and organization, as well as in emphasis, to make the book both more interesting and informative.

Ten years have passed since the publication of our first edition. In the intervening years we have benefited from suggestions and information made by many people, including students, other political scientists, public officials, journalists, and staff members of McGraw-Hill. We wish to express our appreciation for their assistance.

Henry A. Turner

John A. Vieg

CONTENTS

CHAPTER 1

CALIFORNIA, ITS PRIORITIES AND PROBLEMS

Late in the nineteenth century, a brilliant British scholar, Lord Bryce, wrote: "California . . . is in many respects the most striking state in the whole Union, and has more than any other the character of a great country, capable of standing alone in the world." Bryce not only aptly described the state but also prophesied its future. Today California, the most populous state, does indeed have "the character of a great country." Of the more than 125 independent countries, only 25 have populations larger than that of California; and the state's economy surpasses that of any country of the free world except the United States, Germany, Japan, the United Kingdom, and France.

THE GOLDEN STATE

From discovery to statehood

California was named by early Spanish explorers who, when they landed in Lower California, thought it was the mythical "fabulous island of California" west of Mexico, about which the Spanish novelist García Ordóñez de Montalvo had written. The first European known to have set foot on California soil was the Portuguese explorer Juan Rodríguez Cabrillo, who landed at San Diego Bay in 1542, just fifty years after Columbus discovered America. Other explorers followed, but more than two hundred years elapsed before the King of Spain in 1769 ordered settlements to be made at San Diego and Monterey. By 1834, the Franciscans under the leadership of Padre Junípero Serra had founded a total of twenty-one missions along the coast from San Diego to Sonoma, each a day's journey from the next. Military outposts, called presidios, were established to protect the missions; and small towns, called pueblos, grew up around some of the missions and adjacent presidios.

Although Spain was the ruling power, the presidios were far apart and were so lacking in strength that they were unable to prevent Russian explorers from establishing in 1812 a trading post, Fort Ross, less than a hundred miles north of San Francisco. During the Spanish colonial era, a period of about fifty years, California was governed by local authorities under a provincial governor responsible to the Spanish viceroy in Mexico. Spanish rule continued until the Mexican government declared its independence from Spain in 1821.

Although California territory came under Mexico's control, it was not until 1837 that Mexico drew up a new constitution providing a government for the area. This government lasted only nine years before the region came under the authority of American military officials in 1846. During the brief Mexican period, a number of American explorers, fur traders, and business entrepreneurs entered California; and by the time of the outbreak of war between the United States and Mexico in 1846, there was considerable American influence in the area. Mexico formally ceded California to the United States in the Treaty of Guadalupe Hidalgo on February 2, 1848. Meanwhile, just nine days previously and unknown to the signers of the treaty, James W. Marshall had discovered gold at Coloma in the tailrace of Sutter's sawmill. The news of this discovery set off the famous gold rush of the forty-niners. By 1850, when California was admitted to the Union as the thirty-first state, there were already more than 92,000 persons in the area; and the period of Spanish predominance was at an end.

Although certain communities within the state make some effort to preserve its romantic past, the colonial era has left little impact upon California as it is today. Spanish and Mexican land grants resulted in litigation over disputed land titles, and some of the litigation ended only recently. California's community property laws derive from the Spanish legal system. Most other ties with the prestatehood days are nostalgic rather than substantial and are reflected mainly in the widespread use of Spanish names for counties, cities, and streets; the staging of various local fiestas; the restoration of old missions; and the continuing, though diminishing, influence of Spanish architecture.

The land

Extremes, opposites, and contrasts characterize California, which was given by Nature lavish endowments of natural resources. Its territory, larger than that of Britain, Italy, or Japan, is exceeded in size among the states of the Union only by those of Alaska and Texas. Its 1,100-mile Pacific coastline matches the distance from Boston, Massachusetts, to Charleston, South Carolina. Because of its extensive ocean frontage, lofty mountains, fertile valleys, and vast stretches of desert, it has more varieties of climate and of plant and animal life than can be found in any other part of the country.

Three-fourths of the state consists of mountains, foothills, rolling hills, and deserts, varying in elevation from 14,494 feet above sea level to 282 feet below sea level. Most of the people live along the coast or in the valleys on the remaining one-fourth of the land. The Sierra Nevada range extends nearly two-thirds of the eastern length of the state and converges at both ends with the Coast Ranges, which border the Pacific from Washington to Mexico. Between the two ranges lies the flat, fertile Central Valley, extending more than 450 miles north and south and averaging 50 miles in width. California's deserts cover the southeastern portion of the state. Mount Whitney is the nation's tallest peak outside Alaska; Death Valley, only 60 miles away, is the lowest place on the continent. The largest tree in the world stands in Sequoia National Park, while in nearby Yosemite National Park is Yosemite Falls, the highest waterfall in North America.

There is wide diversity, too, in climate—from the dry, extremely hot temperatures at El Centro and Death Valley to the cool breezes and fog of the coastal areas. In the summer, the high peaks of the Sierra Nevada have temperatures similar to those along the coast; in the winter they are covered with snow, and their subzero temperatures are among the coldest in the United States. The snow never melts from the high mountain peaks, and flowers bloom in some places throughout the year.

In most areas of the United States, the four seasons follow each other with marked changes in weather. Much of California is different in that there are essentially only two seasons—the rainy winter and the dry summer. There is, however, tremendous variation in rainfall from north to south in the state. In the north along the coast, some areas have more than 100 inches of rainfall annually, whereas there is pro- gressively less rain farther south with some areas of southeastern Cali- fornia having less than 2 inches of annual rainfall. Hence the thinly populated northern part of the state has a great abundance of water from rainfall and snowfall; but the heavily populated south has vir- tually no snow, little rain, and, consequently, a shortage of water.

The people

The hallmark of the state is its phenomenal growth (see Table 1-1). It had 15,000 people in 1848, and by 1860 it had 380,000. Since then, its population has doubled roughly every twenty years until it has now reached a total of more than 20,000,000. This increase has been due primarily to migration, which has varied from decade to decade de- pending on particular economic, political, and social forces. Economic considerations have invariably been of greatest importance; the largest numbers of immigrants have come during periods of prosperity, the smallest in times of depression.

The gold seekers came first, from every part of the country and from many foreign lands. They were followed by settlers and their families, many of whom came by wagon train. The completion of the

Central Pacific Railroad in 1869 and of the Santa Fe Railroad in the late 1880s made the journey less arduous and encouraged a new influx of immigrants. Thousands were lured west by the claims of land boosters as well as by cheap railway fares, which for a time, because of a rate war between the Santa Fe and the Southern Pacific, were as low as $1 from Kansas City to Los Angeles. World War I and the prosperity of the 1920s triggered new waves of migration. Opportunities in the rapidly expanding oil fields brought some; others were attracted by the developing movie industry, while still others were drawn by the vision of retirement in the sunshine. The 1930s brought refugees from the dust bowls of the Middle West, and during World War II thousands of war workers and servicemen were temporary residents, and many decided to make the Golden State their permanent home. In recent years, the aerospace, electronic, and television industries have been magnets, especially for young adults.

Today California has one-tenth of the population of the entire United States, and the state has accounted for nearly one-fifth of the population growth of the nation since 1960. However, as is shown in Table 1-1, the population growth was less in the 1960s than in the 1950s, due to a decline in migration.

TABLE 1-1   *Population increase by decades*

Date	Population	Increase over prior census	
		NUMERICAL	PERCENT
1850	92,597		
1860	379,994	287,279	310
1870	560,247	180,253	47
1880	864,694	304,447	54
1890	1,213,398	348,704	40
1900	1,485,053	271,655	22
1910	2,377,549	892,496	60
1920	3,426,861	1,049,312	44
1930	5,677,251	2,250,390	66
1940	6,907,387	1,230,133	22
1950	10,586,223	3,678,839	53
1960	15,863,000	5,276,777	49
1970	20,098,863	4,235,863	27

SOURCES: U.S. Department of Commerce, Bureau of the Census, California State Department of Finance.

California's people have diverse origins. Throughout the history of the state, inhabitants born elsewhere have outnumbered the native sons and daughters. Today 44 percent of the state's population was born in California, 10 percent in foreign countries, and the remainder in other states. The native migrants have come from all parts of the country, with the North Central states contributing the largest number—more than 3 million—followed by the Southern states, which have contributed 2,200,000 Californians. Of the foreign-born residents of California, the largest number came from Mexico, followed by Canada, Italy, and England.

California's population has contributed to the state's influential role in national politics. As the most populous state in the nation, it now has the largest delegation in Congress and at the presidential nominating conventions, and it has the largest number of electoral votes. In recent decades, its governors, United States senators, and other political leaders have been potential contenders for their parties' nominations for the Presidency and vice presidency. Except for 1964, a Californian has been nominated for the Presidency or vice presidency in every election since 1948. A native son, Richard Nixon, now serves as the nation's Chief Executive, and more of the top appointive officials are from California than from any other state.

The economy

California's economy reflects its strength in both natural and human resources; it ranks among the leading states in every major field of economic activity. It had more than 8 million people gainfully employed in 1970, and that number is expected to reach 10.4 million by 1980. For several years per capita income in the state has been more than 20 percent above the national average.

NATURAL RESOURCES Mining, California's principal industry during its early years, has continued to be of major importance. Only two states derive more income from this source, in part because no other region of comparable size in the world has a greater variety of mineral deposits of commercial value. Petroleum and its by-products account for roughly three-fourths of the income from mineral resources. Although gold is still mined commercially, in terms of value, it ranks far below such products as cement, boron, clay, sand, and gravel. Lumber and fishing are also important industries; California's lumber industry is exceeded only by that of Oregon, and its income from commercial fishing is higher than that of any other state.

AGRICULTURE   With less than 3 percent of its labor force engaged in farming, California is the leading state in agricultural production. This achievement has been made possible by vast reclamation and irrigation projects, which have converted large areas of desert and sparsely grazed range lands into intensively cultivated farms and ranches. Of the state's total of 100 million acres, the 8 million now under irrigation support 85 percent of all farm production in the state.

In no other state does one find such specialization and diversification in agriculture as in California. The state produces commercial quantities of every major crop grown in the United States, except tobacco. Altogether, 275 farm products are produced for market, of which 269 are agricultural crops and the remainder livestock. Three decades ago oranges were the first ranking crop, but now they rank seventh in market value behind dairy products, beef cattle, cotton, hay, eggs, and grapes. California leads all other states in the production of many crops; and it grows almost all the nation's production of some, such as lemons, walnuts, dates, and olives.

INDUSTRY AND COMMERCE   Its location makes the state the economic gateway to the entire Pacific and Far East; and through its principal harbors (at San Francisco, Los Angeles, and San Diego) moves much of California's foreign trade, which makes it the leading export state.

In terms of the number of persons employed in the state, manufacturing is the leading category, followed by trade, services, and government (see Figure 1-1). Employment in manufacturing has expanded more rapidly than in any other area. Approximately one-third of California's manufacturing employment is in aerospace and defense industries; and, if the federal government sharply reduces its spending in these areas, the level of unemployment in the state may rise higher than elsewhere. Approximately 16 percent of California workers are employed by the federal, state, or local governments. Largely because of the military establishments within its borders, there are more federal employees in California than in any other state or in the District of Columbia.

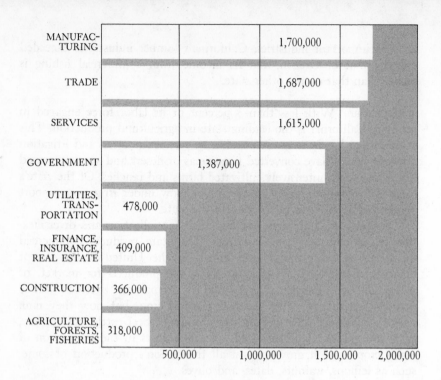

	500,000	1,000,000	1,500,000	2,000,000
MANUFAC-TURING			1,700,000	
TRADE			1,687,000	
SERVICES			1,615,000	
GOVERNMENT		1,387,000		
UTILITIES, TRANS-PORTATION	478,000			
FINANCE, INSURANCE, REAL ESTATE	409,000			
CONSTRUCTION	366,000			
AGRICULTURE, FORESTS, FISHERIES	318,000			

FIGURE 1-1 *Civilian employment in California, 1969* (Economic Report of the Governor, 1970)

PRIORITIES AND PROBLEMS

All of California's priorities and problems are related to its rapidly expanding population. During the two decades before 1970, the state's population increased from 10.6 million to approximately 20 million. No other state or country has experienced such a phenomenal increase in population. In the words of one writer: "In California you are not certain about today, only about tomorrow. Tomorrow will be worse and better but mostly bigger. More crowded and a little less like the California that all of us help to destroy by becoming part of it."[1] According to the latest projections, the state will have a population of approxi-

[1] Neil Morgan, "California, The Nation Within a Nation," *Saturday Review*, Sept. 23, 1967, p. 18.

mately 24 million by 1980, 29 million by 1990, and 34 million by the year 2000. If these predictions materialize, providing sufficient new homes, jobs, recreational facilities, schools and other governmental services and seeking solutions to a variety of related problems are tasks that will require the talents of California's most able citizens.

Planning population growth

California's population has never been evenly distributed throughout the state but has been concentrated in a few areas. Unlike the early settlers in other states, the first migrants to California came not to farm but to search for gold, and from that time to the present the state has had a smaller proportion of rural residents than the nation as a whole. In recent decades, throughout much of the United States there has been a steady population movement from rural to urban areas, but urbanization has advanced further in California than in any other state.

Many of California's problems were created or magnified by the heavy concentration of people in a relatively small proportion of the state. At present, 90 percent of the people live in the state's fourteen metropolitan districts[2] and their twenty-two component counties; hence the remaining thirty-six counties contain only one-tenth of the people. The trend toward metropolitan living is continuing. Nine out of every ten of the persons added to California's population since 1950 live in metropolitan regions, and nearly two-thirds of that growth has been in southern California. Half of those gainfully employed in California work within a 60-mile radius of downtown Los Angeles. Of the recent metropolitan growth, 80 percent of the increase has occurred in suburbs and only 20 percent in the central city. This suburban development is one of the important population trends in California.

Demographers predict that, unless positive actions are taken soon, by the year 2000 there will be a gigantic megalapolis, which they label San-San, extending from San Diego to San Francisco. What this might mean in terms of total congestion is virtually beyond comprehension. One newspaper editorialized: "If California continues merely to stumble into tomorrow, letting things happen as if the worst in Megalopolis is

[2] The U.S. Census Bureau defines a metropolitan area as a "county or a group of contiguous counties which contain at least one city of 50,000 inhabitants or more."

ordained and beyond the solution of man—California, the wonderland, will become California, the nightmare."[3]

Until recently, most Californians have taken pride in the state's spectacular growth and have given little thought either to the consequences of such growth or to plans for directing it. Some people, however, have begun to realize the problems inherent in uncontrolled population growth. As a result, several proposals have been advanced for reversing the trend toward further population increases in metropolitan areas. Environmentalists in general urge that concerted efforts be made to stabilize the population and that the objective of zero population growth be substituted for the idea that "bigger" is the key to progress. Asserting that the emphasis should be on quality and not quantity, they are attempting to counteract propaganda for a "greater California" by emphasizing the advantages of a "lesser California."

Although there is increasing concern over the dangers in rapid growth, many people see no way of stabilizing California's population in the near future and insist that steps should be taken to plan for future population increases. Some have suggested that a number of planned cities be developed away from presently congested areas. For instance, it has been proposed that five or six cities, each of approximately 250,000 population, be established along the California Aqueduct, which will carry water down the west side of the San Joaquin Valley. Some people, hoping to discourage further migration into southern California, are proposing that no additional water be transported south, arguing that migrants be encouraged to settle in the north.

In 1970, Governor Ronald Reagan's Environmental Quality Study Council issued a report urging the adoption of a statewide population distribution policy. It included among its recommendations that all major public works programs, such as freeways and water distribution systems, be considered from the standpoint of their impact on the development of "dehumanized, sprawling megalopolitan monsters," and that population support facilities—such as transportation, power, and water—be established in sparsely populated regions in order to attract industry and people. The council recognized, however, that it would require "superhuman political will" to counteract the trend toward further congestion in the state's metropolitan areas.

[3] *Sacramento Bee*, Mar. 20, 1969.

Preserving and renewing the environment

California's increasing population necessitates that positive steps be taken to preserve and renew the environment. As mentioned earlier, there is urgent need to reduce and direct California's future growth; there is also need to focus attention on the extent to which man has spoiled his environment with urban congestion, noise, garbage, noxious chemicals, fumes, sewage, and industrial wastes.

Plans for future developments should be based on consideration of the concept of social costs, which are the negative consequences for society that result from actions of private individuals or government. For example, the long-range social costs of the mechanization of farming include the added congestion in cities caused by displaced farm workers. Some critics of the California Water Plan contend that it entails a number of social costs that will have to be paid in the future when southern California is even more congested and more polluted than it is now and when ecological damage has resulted from moving water from the north to the south.

In 1970, the Assembly Select Committee on Environmental Quality outlined a 5-billion-dollar, ten-year program aimed at protecting and revitalizing the environment. It urged the adoption of a constitutional amendment providing a legal basis for controlling where people may live and how they may use their land, establishment of local and regional planning agencies, coordination of statewide environmental control policies, control over all public and private developments along the coast to prevent destruction of resources, and establishment of a 250-million-dollar, five-year program to buy open spaces and undeveloped beaches. The implementation of this program should have the support of all people in the state.

AIR POLLUTION Air pollution is a problem for virtually every industrial city in the world. Possibly in no place is it a more critical issue than in California, and especially in the Los Angeles area.

Although various steps have been taken in California to combat the menace of smog, the air steadily becomes more contaminated. During the first half of 1970, Los Angeles had more smog alerts than in any previous comparable period. The U.S. Forest Service has reported that more than 1.3 million trees in the San Bernardino National Forest are

"That's not an enemy attack, children—those are friendly fellow-Americans" (Reprinted by permission of Herblock)

dying from the effects of smog. The effect of smog on visibility may be seen as far as 150 miles east of the coast, and the deaths of livestock up to 35 miles from San Francisco have been attributed to air pollution.

Chemical analysis of pollutants escaping into the air in the Los Angeles basin indicates that while some of the impurities are caused by industrial installations such as power plants, oil refineries, painting and cleaning establishments, and aviation plants, the major sources are automobiles and trucks. In the two largest metropolitan regions in particular, the construction of mass rapid transit systems capable of moving hundreds of thousands of people not only would reduce the danger of smog but also would relieve traffic congestion.

The Los Angeles Air Pollution Control District (APCD) has the strictest smog regulations in the world. Yet, while they have been able to prevent tons of impurities from escaping into the atmosphere every day, the growth of population in the Los Angeles area has been so great that it has largely offset the effect of these restrictions. Professor Paul Ehrlich relates smog to the basic problem of overpopulation: "Smog may be caused by too many cars, but . . . too many cars are caused by too many people."[4] In any event, more stringent and effective measures against air pollution should be adopted immediately and should be enforced by the federal, state, and local governments.

WATER POLLUTION AND WATER DISTRIBUTION   California's water problems are of two basic types: pollution and distribution. The first is the handiwork of man; the second is caused by the vagaries of nature.

Water pollution   California's waters have long had pollutants dumped into them, but relatively little effort was made to attack the problem until the 1960s. With the rapid increase in population and industrial development, many local sewage treatment plants have been taxed beyond their designed capacities; and more wastes continue to be discharged into the streams, lakes, and bays. For example, in 1969 the pollution problem became so grave along the waters and beaches of the Monterey Peninsula that along 6 miles of beaches the county health officer posted signs warning against swimming. Action has been taken, usually on the initiative of the State Water Resources Control Board

[4] Paul R. Ehrlich, *The Population Bomb*, New York, Ballantine Books, Inc., 1968, p. 179.

or regional boards, to end or greatly reduce the polluting of such varied waters as Lake Tahoe, San Francisco Bay, and Los Angeles Harbor. Legislation enacted in 1969 provided for penalties of $6,000 per day for water polluters, and in 1970 a bond issue was approved to match funds provided by the federal government to reduce water pollution by improving local sewage-treatment plants. In endorsing this proposal, Governor Reagan commented that "water polluters" had been put on notice by the State Water Resources Control Board that long delays in correcting "water-quality abuses will not be tolerated" and that the adoption of the bond issues could "once again make California's waters clean and clear,"[5] a prediction all Californians doubtless hope will be realized.

Long-lived noxious chemicals (such as DDT) used as pesticides are proving to be serious water pollutants. One unexpected result or social cost of the pollution of the ocean in this manner has been the reduction in the number of seabirds, which, after eating contaminated fish, are unable to produce hard-shelled eggs that will hatch. In 1970, there were fewer than one-half the normal number of young pelicans along the coast, and other species such as the cormorant and murre are also affected.

With the installation of oil-drilling platforms off the coast of southern California, the possibility of a new and unusually serious type of pollution became a reality—oil pollution of the coastal waters and beaches. In January, 1969, an oil blowout occurred at one of the platforms a few miles off the coast of Santa Barbara; and for months oil flowed to the surface, spreading over more than 800 square miles of ocean and washing on the beaches from north of Santa Barbara to Santa Monica. Offshore oil drilling was stopped for a few weeks but was later resumed despite the efforts of certain elected officials and conservation groups to end all drilling along the coast permanently. Few individuals doubt that as long as offshore drilling is permitted, other oil blowouts and further pollution of the water and beaches will occur.

Water distribution In addition to having a coastline of nearly 1,100 miles, California has within its borders 3,000 square miles of rivers, lakes, bays, and harbors. Although many areas have insufficient rainfall, the state's water supply is adequate for the present and for the foreseeable future. Hence the principal problem is that of distribution.

[5] *Los Angeles Times,* July 26, 1970, sec. G, p. 5.

In the northern mountainous third of the state, where approximately three-quarters of the rainfall occurs, the trouble generally is too much water or too fast a runoff and possible flooding. In the middle and southern portions of the state, where the great majority of the people reside, there is a chronic water shortage. To provide the water required for urban and industrial needs and for the irrigation of farmland, scores of dams, canals, and aqueducts have been constructed during the past sixty years.[6] The California Water Project, started in 1957 after a decade of planning, is the largest and most important public works undertaking in the history of the state. When in full operation it is designed to deliver 4.2 million acre-feet of water annually from northern to central and southern California. When the project is entirely completed it will include twenty dams and reservoirs, twenty-four pumping stations, eight power plants, and 580 miles of canals and tunnels. A central element is the California Aqueduct, a "cement river" 30 feet deep, which will run from near the Sacramento–San Joaquin Delta to Lake Perris, east of Los Angeles (see Figure 1-2). The California Water Project has encountered considerable opposition from the time it was first conceived. Governor Edmund G. "Pat" Brown, over much resistance from northern Californians who objected to having water originating in their area transported south, secured legislative approval of the project in 1959 and the next year obtained voter approval of a massive 1.7-billion-dollar bond issue to finance its construction. Opposition, however, has continued both from northern Californians and from other people who are fearful of possible detrimental ecological effects, especially in the Sacramento–San Joaquin Delta region.

The development of these vast water potentialities represents a tremendous undertaking, not only in engineering and finance, but also from the standpoint of equitable treatment of all regions and groups of people in the state. Several major issues remain to be settled, including: What preference, if any, should be accorded publicly owned and operated utility systems in the sale of hydroelectric power produced by the

[6] The largest of these are the 238-mile Owens River Aqueduct (1913) and the Mono Lake Extension (1940), which supply water for the city of Los Angeles; San Francisco's 135-mile Hetch-Hetchy Aqueduct (1934); the Metropolitan Water District's 242-mile aqueduct from the Parker Dam on the Colorado River to Los Angeles and San Diego (1941); and the Hoover, Pardee, Shasta, Friant, and Pine Flat dams.

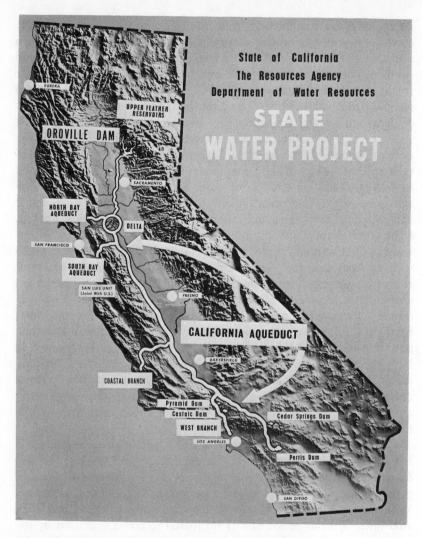

FIGURE 1-2 *California Water Project, the greatest public works undertaking in the history of any state*

various dams? What kinds of restrictions should be imposed on the sale of water to preclude "unjust enrichment" of a few at the expense of the many? What additional measures should be taken to safeguard the Delta from intrusion of salt water through the Carquinez Straits? How can northern California be assured of the natural development of its own economy while exporting large quantities of water annually to insure the further growth of southern California? Finally, to what extent is further growth in southern California desirable?

Racial equality

Another major goal for Californians is the achievement of social, economic, and political equality for all the state's inhabitants. Unfortunately, discrimination is found in most countries or regions populated by people of diverse religious or racial backgrounds,[7] and California is no exception. Virtually every ethnic group is represented in California. There are four important minority groups in the state, whose members in general do not share fully in the economic and political life of the state. Of these, the most numerous are people with Spanish surnames, usually called Mexican-Americans, although some prefer the term "Chicanos."[8] In 1967, 11 percent of the state's inhabitants were Mexican-Americans, their numbers having increased from 760,453 in 1950 to 1,425,538 in 1960 and to 2,162,100 in 1967.

Blacks comprise the second largest minority group. In 1967, they constituted 7 percent of the state's population. Their number in the state has increased from 462,172 in 1950 to 883,361 in 1960 and to 1,402,400 in 1967. This is the largest percentage increase among all population groupings during the past two decades. The heaviest concentrations of blacks and Mexican-Americans are in Los Angeles County. In fact, there are more people with Spanish surnames in the city of Los Angeles than in any other city in North America except Mexico City.

The third largest ethnic category consists of those individuals with Asian ancestry. In 1967, they numbered 389,600, or 2 percent of the population. The fourth group, the American Indians, although con-

[7] For example, various religious, racial, or ethnic groups have been subjected to discrimination in Belgium, Ireland, Canada, India, South Africa, the Soviet Union, and various other countries.
[8] The term "Chicano" has been defined as meaning "a Mexican-American with a non-Anglo image of himself." Ruben Salazar, "Who Is a Chicano? And What Is It the Chicanos Want?" Los Angeles Times, Feb. 6, 1970.

siderably smaller in numbers than the other three groups, has also grown substantially in recent years, from approximately 20,000 in 1950 to 39,014 in 1960 and 58,400 in 1967.

Today, people of Asian descent are generally more fully assimi-

"Pattern for Chaos," highlighting the danger inherent in the greater-than-average unemployment of minority groups (Reprinted by permission of Newton Pratt and the Sacramento Bee)

lated socially and economically than are members of the other three minority groups; however, in the past, both the Chinese-Americans and Japanese-Americans have been subject to special kinds of discrimination. For instance, one entire article of the 1879 state constitution was devoted to the Chinese; it prohibited their employment on public works or by corporations and authorized the legislature to adopt measures prohibiting further Chinese immigration. Although the United States Supreme Court ruled in due course that the article was unconstitutional, it was not until 1952 that these provisions were removed from the California constitution by a vote of the people. Possibly the most obvious example of an ethnic group being singled out for discriminatory treatment is the relocation of the Japanese by the federal government during World War II.

During the past decade, the blacks and Mexican-Americans and, to a lesser extent, the Indians have engaged in various forms of social protest to indicate dissatisfaction with their economic and political status. Their demands have included better and integrated public schools, increased opportunities for higher education, the establishment of black studies and Mexican-American studies departments at colleges and universities, the ending of discrimination in employment, more satisfactory welfare programs, and greater political representation.[9] Most Californians would approve of these aspirations, although many do not agree with some of the methods employed to achieve them. California, the largest state in the nation and with a highly diversified population, should be a leader in resolving the issue of racial equality. Experience suggests that the possibility of resort to violence tends to be greatest, not where the differences in income and living conditions between races are greatest, but rather where the gap has been reduced to the point that the disadvantaged are tempted to gamble on the chance that a dramatic effort might eliminate the gap altogether. This psychological fact offers at least a partial explanation for the Watts riots in August, 1965, and also for the increasing determination of Mexican-Americans and Indians to organize for the fulfillment of their demands. Clearly,

[9] In 1970, the California Legislature included one Mexican-American, two members of Asian descent, and six blacks, one of whom, John L. Miller, was chosen by the Democrats as their floor leader in the assembly. Wilson Riles, who was elected superintendent of public instruction in 1970, became the first black to be elected to a major statewide office.

one of the great challenges of this age concerns the difficulty of getting people with different ethnic and religious backgrounds to make the adjustments necessary if they are to live and work together harmoniously.

Beleaguered education

Education is the principal activity of California state and local governments. No other public function in the state involves so many people or consumes so much state and local revenue. Moreover, its social consequences overshadow those of all other governmental programs, for education has been the primary means of economic and social upward mobility for millions of people. Much of the greatness of the state (and nation) may be attributed to its publicly supported schools and colleges.

In the past, California has had as good a system of public education as any state in the nation and the broadest, and probably the best, system of tax-supported higher education—city colleges, state colleges, and the nine-campus state university. In recent years, however, both California public schools and its colleges and university have encountered major difficulties. The principal problems confronting public education include obtaining adequate financing, achieving an adjustment of the various ethnic groups in integrated schools, and developing curricula designed to meet the needs of young people living in a swiftly changing world. The financial crisis of the public schools stems largely from the defeat by the voters of local bond and tax measures and from the failure of the state government to provide additional funds.

The problems of the state colleges and the state university are so extraordinarily complicated that there is the danger in any brief discussion of misleading oversimplification. There is little question, however, that the state colleges and the university have suffered in recent years from inadequate financing. For example, in terms of per capita financial support for the state university, California ranks thirtieth in the nation and eleventh among the thirteen Western states. From the standpoint of faculty salaries, the state university slipped from tenth among the nation's colleges and universities in the early 1960s to forty-third by 1970; and state college salaries were lower yet.[10] Because of insufficient funding for new construction and for hiring additional

[10] *Los Angeles Times*, Feb. 4, 1970, pt. II, p. 4, and July 12, 1970, sec. C, p. 1.

faculty members, some qualified students have been denied admission to institutions of their choice. Space limitations do not permit a discussion of the various ramifications and probable consequences of low budgets for the college and university campuses.

Higher education in California no longer has the same degree of public support it enjoyed a few years ago. While several events and developments have led to this growing estrangement of higher education and the general public, a major factor has been student demonstrations. In June, 1970, the Gallup Poll reported that a majority of the American people considered campus unrest the nation's leading problem, ranking it as even more serious than such issues as the Vietnam war or racial strife. The fact that such demonstrations have occurred at colleges and universities in more than fifty countries indicates that student unrest is a worldwide phenomenon and is not limited to California or even the United States. On the positive side, it should be regarded as a healthy sign that college students show an interest in such problems as racial inequality, poverty, and international affairs. Nevertheless, a number of California campuses have been seriously disrupted by demonstrations, strikes, physical violence, the burning of buildings, bomb threats, and actual bombings.

Undoubtedly, only a small proportion of students and faculty are responsible for initiating such actions. According to a survey of the Educational Testing Service, the radical element on American campuses constitutes only about 2 percent of the student body, although many moderates may support demonstrations on specific issues. Undoubtedly, the students involved have been motivated by a variety of factors. In some instances, the disturbances have been magnified by overreaction of police and other officials and by the efforts of certain elected officials to gain personal political advantages. The university has also suffered because of actions of nonstudents. For example, of 674 demonstrators arrested by campus police at Berkeley in the first six months of 1970, only 87 were enrolled in the university. According to the chief of campus police, "events often attributed to Berkeley do not relate to the university" but are the results of "street actions" by nonstudents. Most students and faculty members would agree that colleges and universities should be neither isolated citadels of learning nor instruments for revolutionary change. Instead, a proper balance should be sought between the search for knowledge and concern for social change.

Related to campus disturbances is a basic question—who should make the controlling decisions regarding academic life? With regard to what issues should the boards of trustees or regents have final authority? What powers should be exercised by campus administrators and what decisions should be made by faculties? Finally, what should be the character of student relationships to their colleges? Regarding the latter question, the former quasi-parental relationship assumed by college officials toward students is no longer appropriate, but certain standards of conduct obviously should govern students' relationships with each other, the faculty, and the administration. Although some questions must be left to deliberation and decision by those professionally qualified to make the necessary judgments, there is growing agreement that students should be involved in academic decision making where appropriate and in particular in matters related to academic programs and to campus life.

Responsible political leadership

Although many of California's problems can be resolved by private groups and individuals, the solutions for the more complex and important issues require the efforts of government and the leadership of far-sighted, responsible public officials. The importance of leadership is often underestimated. Particularly during times of crises such as California has recently experienced, leaders must play major roles in seeking answers to complicated political problems and in resolving social conflicts. The responsible political leader acknowledges that there may be honest and honorable differences of opinion on public issues.

One task of present-day leadership in California is to encourage and to enable greater participation in the political processes by all citizens and especially by those most likely to feel alienated from the political system. Apparently, these include many of the young people of the state as well as some members of minority groups. Generally, since the time of Governor Hiram W. Johnson—and especially during the long tenure of Earl Warren as governor—California has had a political climate of moderation and good will, the atmosphere of what might be called *the politics of reason and responsibility*. For the most part, during the past two generations, California has been governed by political leaders whose approach to public problems has been moderate. Their disposition has been to accept in good faith what their predecessors have done and to attempt to build new programs on what had gone before. The principal test they have applied has been one of results: Have the policies and programs of the government as carried out in practice produced tangible benefits for the people of the state? This has been California's political tradition and it is a valuable heritage: not government by dogma but government in response to what Justice Oliver Wendell Holmes called "the felt necessities of the times."

"What is past is prologue"

The foregoing are by no means the only problems confronting California. Other important issues include controlling crime, juvenile delinquency, and drug use; establishing mass rapid transit systems for metropolitan areas; modernizing state and local governments, especially those in metropolitan areas; facilitating the solutions of labor-management problems, including those related to migratory workers; and combating unemployment and inflation. In the following chapters various proposals for improving California government will be discussed.

Most accounts of California in the past have emphasized the positive aspects of the state—its abundance of natural resources, appealing climate, expanding economy, and growing population. Typically, California has been depicted as a land of opportunity and promise, with few serious problems. Recently, more and more people have focused on the shortcomings and disadvantages of the state and have often overlooked the favorable features. According to David Riesman, a distinguished political sociologist, Californians tend to be victims of "masochistic narcissism—the idea that you are either the greatest or the worst." The desired approach obviously is to view the state with a realistic, balanced perspective, overestimating neither its outstanding qualities nor its problems.

Each of the states has a distinct personality stemming from its history, geography, economy, people, and problems. It has been the purpose of this chapter to sketch briefly salient facts that have an influence upon California politics and government. The hallmark of the state has been change and phenomenal growth, both of which will probably continue. In the Golden State, "What is past is prologue."

CHAPTER 2

☾HE CONSTITUTION AND
DIRECT DEMOCRACY

Under American federalism, each state must operate in accordance with the basic law established by the national Constitution and its own constitution. The former, in addition to providing for the organized structure of the national government, divides governmental powers between the nation and the states and places certain obligations and limitations on both levels of government. The United States Constitution does not attempt to specify what functions a state may perform. Instead, it provides, in the Tenth Amendment, that powers not delegated to the national government, "nor prohibited by it to the states, are reserved to the states respectively, or to the people." Thus, except for the few restrictions set forth in the national Constitution, every state is free to draft whatever type of constitution it desires and to change it at any time.

In theory, a constitution is a body of organic law providing for both the machinery of the government and the protection of the people against any arbitrary exercise of authority. It should consist of the fundamental principles upon which the government is founded, principles not subject to frequent change but representing the cumulative wisdom of the past. Governmental details and matters of an ephemeral or transitory nature should not be placed in the constitution but should be left to the discretion of legislative and executive officials. The United States Constitution is an excellent example of what a constitution should be. Unfortunately, the California constitution is not; although considerably improved through recent revisions, it still includes much material that is statutory in character.

THE CALIFORNIA CONSTITUTION

The constitution of 1849

The framers of California's first constitution, meeting at Monterey from September 1 to October 13, 1849, relied heavily on the constitutions of other states. What they produced was less an original document than a compilation of sections borrowed from several other state constitutions. Approximately half of the provisions were taken from the Iowa constitution adopted three years earlier, and a number of others came from the New York constitution.

In organizing the government, the separation-of-powers principle was followed, and three branches were established: executive, legislative, and judicial. Unlike the federal government, however, in which the President and the Vice President are the only executive officials, provision was made for the election of most of the state's executive officers.

On November 13, 1849, the voters approved the constitution and at the same time elected the state's officers, two congressmen, and two United States senators. Nearly a year elapsed, however, before Congress, by accepting the principles of the Compromise of 1850, admitted California to the Union as the thirty-first state. The date of this vote, September 9, is celebrated in California as Admission Day.

It became evident soon after the constitution of 1849 went into effect that the document was not adequate for the booming state. During the next quarter century, California's population grew from 90,000 to 860,000 persons and the state underwent a remarkable transformation in commerce, industry, transportation, and agriculture. These developments were accompanied by problems of similar magnitude. Corruption in government was widespread. The Southern Pacific Railroad gained a stranglehold on a large part of the state; the importation of Chinese workers resulted in an explosive labor and racial situation; much of the land was controlled by a few owners; and the farmers and laborers believed that they were at the mercy of banks and other corporate "monopolists." In the mid-1870s an economic depression, intensified by a prolonged drought, magnified the state's problems and brought them into sharper focus.

During this period the legislature on four occasions submitted to the voters the question of calling a convention to write a new and more satisfactory constitution, but it was not until 1877 that the electorate approved the proposal. Early the next year, the legislature provided for the election of delegates and stipulated that they should convene in Sacramento on September 28, 1878. After sessions lasting about six months, the convention adjourned on March 3, 1879, and shortly thereafter the electorate adopted the proposed new constitution by a majority of less than 11,000 out of a total of 145,000 votes.

The constitution of 1879

A comparison of the constitutions of 1849 and 1879 reveals that the framers of the latter document did not draft an entirely new constitution but retained a number of sections that were in the one which preceded it. Because of the interest in social and economic reforms, the delegates placed in the constitution detailed and specific provisions, many of which were of a legislative nature. The most striking difference in the new document was its length: it was three times as long as the first constitution.

Much of the increase resulted from the efforts of the delegates to strike at the specific sources of discontent of that day. A commission was created to regulate railroads, and the Board of Equalization was established to equalize property valuations in the various counties and to assess railroad property. The low esteem in which public officials were held is indicated by the restrictions placed on all three branches of government. The legislature, in particular, was placed under a number of limitations, many of them having to do with special legislation and state finance. Various parts of the constitution will be discussed in subsequent chapters.

Amending the constitution

THE AMENDING PROCESS   Two steps are required to amend the California constitution: (1) an amendment must be proposed, and (2) it must be ratified. An amendment may be proposed either by the legislature or, through the initiative, by a group of voters. For an amendment to be proposed by the legislature, it must be approved by a two-thirds vote of the elected members of each house. To propose an amendment by the initiative, a petition requesting the action must be signed by voters equal in number to 8 percent of those voting for the office of governor in the preceding election. (The initiative process will be discussed later in this chapter.) Any amendment, however proposed, must be placed on the ballot at the following general election, and if approved by a majority of the electorate voting on that proposition, it is ratified and becomes a part of the constitution. Of the 385 constitutional amendments adopted by 1971, 362 had originated with the legislature and 23 through the initiative. (See Figure 2-1.)

WHY SO MANY AMENDMENTS?   California has had the dubious distinction of having the third longest constitution in the United States. It is nearly twice as long as that of any other state, except those of Alabama and Louisiana, which are longer yet. Although the size of California's constitution is partly due to the original length, much of its bulk is due to supplementary material added through amendment.

The California constitution has been amended more times than that of any other state. Why? The explanation is simple. A comparison of the basic document with those of other states reveals that there is a close relationship between the initial length of a constitution and the frequency with which it has to be changed. A long constitution requires frequent amendment to adjust its detailed provisions to unforeseen and changing conditions.

The growth of the document has also been due in part to the efforts of organized groups to protect or promote their special interests

80647

Assembly Constitutional Amendment   No. 2

Introduced by Assemblymen Briggs, Badham,
Vasconcellos, and Sieroty

January 5, 1971

HELD AT DESK

Assembly Constitutional Amendment No. 2—A resolution to propose to the people of the State of California an amendment to the Constitution of the state, by adding Section 27 to Article I, by amending Section 1 of Article II, and by amending and renumbering Section 22 of Article XX as amended by the people November 6, 1956, relating to the age of majority.

LEGISLATIVE COUNSEL'S DIGEST

ACA 2, as introduced, Briggs (H.A.D.). Age of majority.

Amends Sec. 1, Art. II; Sec. 22, Art. XX, Cal. Const., adds Sec. 27 to Art. I, Cal. Const.

Changes the age of majority from twenty-one years to eighteen years.

Renumbers Sec. 22 of Art. XX as Sec. 21.5.

Vote—⅔; Appropriation—No; Fiscal Committee—No.

1   *Resolved by the Assembly, the Senate concurring,* That the
2   Legislature of the State of California at its 1971 Regular Ses-
3   sion commencing on the fourth day of January, 1971, two-
4   thirds of the members elected to each of the two houses of the
5   Legislature voting therefor, hereby proposes to the people of
6   the State of California that the Constitution of the state be
7   amended by:
8   First—That Section 27 is added to Article I, to read:
9   SEC. 27. The age of majority in California is 18 years.
10   This section shall become operative January 1, 1972.
11   Second—That Section 1 of Article II is amended to read:
12   SECTION 1. Every native citizen of the United States of
13   America, every person who shall have acquired the rights of
14   citizenship under and by virtue of the Treaty of Queretaro,
15   and every naturalized citizen thereof, who shall have become
16   such ninety days prior to any election, of the age of 21 18
17   years, who shall have been a resident of the State one year

FIGURE 2-1   *Assembly constitutional amendment. A senate or assembly constitutional amendment must be approved by two-thirds of the elected membership of each house in order to be submitted to the voters for ratification*

by writing into the constitution provisions of a statutory nature. Some of these groups have experienced little difficulty in getting the legislature to propose amendments desired by them. The ease with which the constitution may be amended by the initiative has also contributed to the amount of legislation frozen into the constitution by organized interests. As previously noted, however, amendments approved through the initiative comprise only a small proportion of the total number adopted.

Other factors, many related to the length and detailed nature of the constitution, have also contributed to the proliferation of amendments. At times, it has been necessary to amend the constitution to grant the legislature needed powers. Some amendments have been adopted to overrule adverse court decisions. Still other amendments have been adopted to provide for governmental reforms such as the civil service system and the executive budget.

Disadvantages of a long constitution

Approximately a decade ago, the chief justice of the California Supreme Court described the state constitution as "cumbersome, unelastic and outmoded." He added, "It is not only much too long, but it is almost everything a constitution ought not to be."

Briefly, what are the principal disadvantages of such a constitution? First, a long constitution is rigid and multiplies the problems of all three branches of government. The work of the courts is increased because the numerous provisions of a bulky constitution present more opportunities for legislation to conflict with it than would a less detailed constitution. Constitutional limitations make it difficult for the legislature, the policy-determining branch, to develop a comprehensive, balanced program for the state. Executive officials are likewise handicapped by detailed provisions which place undesirable limitations on their authority and freedom of action. For example, the governor is responsible for coordinating the administrative agencies of the state; yet due to insufficient authority, as well as the manner in which the executive branch is organized, he is unable to carry out this responsibility effectively.

Second, because of the great amount of legislation written into the constitution, there is now little distinction between statutory and constitutional law. For example, one section of the constitution guarantees the right of a jury trial while another exempts from taxation all nut-bearing trees under four years of age! Obviously, these two provisions are not of equal importance and should not have the same status. Furthermore, because of the length and excessive detail of the document, it is difficult to determine exactly what the constitution provides on several important subjects. For instance, the index to the constitution contains more than 180 entries under the headings of *Taxation* and *Taxes*.

Possibly the most apparent disadvantage of the California constitution has been that it has increased the burden of the voters. Because of the detailed provisions of the constitution, matters which should be settled by the legislature must be referred to the electorate, who may not always be sufficiently informed to render an intelligent judgment. In a general election, the voter may expect to find on the ballot from twelve to more than twenty constitutional amendments, many of them long, technical, and complicated.

Revising the constitution

A thorough revision of the California constitution may be undertaken either by calling a constitutional convention or by establishing a constitutional revision commission. The procedure for calling a constitutional convention is set forth in the constitution: (1) Two-thirds of the elected members of each house of the legislature must approve a resolution for a convention and propose to the voters at the next general election that a convention be called. (2) A majority of the electorate voting on the proposal must favor calling the convention. (3) The legislature at the following session must provide for the convention and the election of delegates. (4) Within three months of the election of the delegates, they must convene to draft the constitution. (5) The proposed new constitution must be submitted to the voters at a special election.

ATTEMPTS TO CALL A CONVENTION On five occasions — 1898, 1914, 1920, 1930, and 1934 — the legislature submitted to the electorate proposals for calling a convention to revise the 1879 constitution. The first four times the propositions were defeated, but in 1934 the electors voted in favor of a convention, which, ironically, was never held, for the legislature failed to pass the necessary enabling legislation. In the 1935 legislative session, the contention was made that as it was not feasible to hold the convention within the time specified by the ballot proposition, no convention need be called then or later. Many observers disagreed with this view; they held that the principal reason the legislators failed to act was their belief that a period of major economic depression was not a propitious time for a constitutional convention.

Evidently the failure of the legislators in recent years to propose calling a convention has been largely due to their fears that a constitutional convention might open a virtual Pandora's box of political problems. For example, the demands of pressure groups for special favors would raise a host of problems; every interest group that has provisions in the constitution granting them special privileges, funds, or protection would undoubtedly converge on the convention, demanding that these privileges be retained. If a constitutional convention succeeded in drafting a model constitution, there still would be a major hurdle in securing its ratification over the combined opposition of the various organized groups.

THE CALIFORNIA CONSTITUTION REVISION COMMISSION Because of the difficulties inherent in changing a constitution by means of a convention, constitutional commissions have been utilized to revise constitutions in several states, among them Florida, Georgia, and Pennsylvania, as well as California. Under this plan, the usual procedure is for the legislature to establish a commission composed mainly of private citizens to draft and present to the legislature a revision of all or part of the state's basic law. The legislature then, with or without modification, submits these recommendations as a constitutional amendment or amendments to the voters.

Although reluctant to propose a constitutional convention, the legislature has created several constitutional revision committees or commissions, the most important of which is the Constitution Revision Commission serving during the years 1963 to 1970. This commission was composed of approximately fifty distinguished lay members and twenty members of the legislature. Assisted by a staff of attorneys and occasionally by expert consultants, it did most of the work through a series of committees, each of which was asked to study a particular article. Proposed revisions to be adopted had to be approved by a two-thirds vote of each house of the legislature and submitted to the voters the same as any other constitutional amendment.

Early in 1966, the commission transmitted to the legislature its recommendations for revising the articles relating to the executive, legislative, and judicial branches of the state government. They involved only one important substantive proposal: that the members of the legislature, like the members of Congress, should be empowered to set their own salaries. Otherwise, they simply rephrased more lucidly the essential provisions of the articles and reduced them from 22,000 to 6,000 words. The legislature submitted these recommendations to the voters in the fall of 1966 practically without change, and they were approved by a wide margin, resulting in the most significant change in the constitution since its adoption in 1879.

Much to the surprise of most commission members, however, their second set of recommendations, although approved by the legislature, was rejected by the voters in the 1968 election. These proposals would have revised in a similar way the articles relating to local government, corporations, public utilities, the civil service, and public education, and would have made the office of superintendent of public instruction appointive rather than elective. Evidently the defeat of this second series of proposals was due to several factors: public apathy, the conservatism of the voters in 1968, overconfidence on the part of the supporters of the amendments, and opposition to changing the method of selecting the superintendent of public instruction.

In 1970, California voters were presented with two sets of propositions embodying constitutional amendments, one in June and one in November. Those recommended by the Constitution Revision Commission at the primary election were in substance almost the same as those that had been defeated in 1968. They were submitted as four separate constitutional amendments, only one of which was adopted; it condensed and clarified the article relating to local government.

At the general election the electorate voted on the final "package" of recommendations formulated by the commission. The four propositions that were approved simplified the section on the state civil service and removed a few positions from the civil service; allowed the legislature to withdraw or change a proposed constitutional amendment after it had been adopted by the legislators but before submission to the voters; and removed obsolete language from the constitution, including provisions relating to social welfare and dueling. One of the defeated propositions would have permitted the use of gas tax moneys for building rapid transit facilities and for controlling smog caused by motor vehicles.

DIRECT DEMOCRACY—THE INITIATIVE AND REFERENDUM

The legislature has the primary responsibility for constitutional amendment and law enactment; however, through the initiative and the referendum, California voters may participate directly in both amending the constitution and enacting laws.[1] The initiative permits the voters to propose and adopt either a constitutional amendment or ordinary legislation; the referendum allows them to suspend a statute adopted by the legislature until it has been approved by the electorate itself. These two devices of direct democracy, along with the recall, were instituted by the Progressives in 1911 under the leadership of Governor Hiram Johnson.

The initiative

Two kinds of initiatives are available in California, constitutional and statutory. The initiative enables a specified number of voters to petition for placement on the ballot either a statute or constitutional amendment and to have it adopted if approved by a majority of the electorate.

For constitutional or statutory initiatives alike, the first step is the drafting of a proposal and the submission of it to the attorney general, who prepares a statement known as the *circulation title*. For a constitutional amendment to qualify for a place on the ballot, the petition must be signed by qualified voters equal in number to 8 percent of the votes cast in the preceding gubernatorial election. The number of signatures required for a statutory initiative is 5 percent.

Actually, there is only one advantage to the constitutional initiative over a statutory initiative: It becomes a part of the state constitution and as such cannot be declared unconstitutional because it conflicts with the state constitution. (It may, however, be invalidated because of conflict with the federal Constitution.) On the other hand, a statu-

[1] Twenty other states provide for the initiative and referendum.

tory initiative measure may be declared unconstitutional if it is found to be in conflict with the provisions of the state constitution. For a group favoring a proposal, the statutory initiative does, however, have this advantage over a law enacted by the legislature: Unless it contains a specific provision to the contrary, a statutory initiative may neither be amended nor be repealed except with the approval of the voters.

Because of the heavy expense involved in getting an initiative proposition on the ballot and securing its adoption, most groups sponsoring statutory measures first try to gain their ends through legislative action. Some groups have, however, preferred to use the initiative process in order to make sure that "their" measures could not later be amended or repealed by the legislature.

The petition referendum

Two general types of referendums are employed in California, *compulsory* and *petition*. Compulsory referendums are required for a new state constitution and all constitutional amendments proposed by the legislature, as well as for state bond issues, city and county charters, and amendments to such charters. All these must be submitted to the voters. Strictly speaking, however, the term "referendum" is not usually applied to those instances in which the action originates in the legislature; it is used only to apply to the petition of "protest" referendum originating with the people.

If, before a statute goes into effect, voters equal to 5 percent of the number casting ballots in the previous gubernatorial election sign a petition protesting the enactment of the measure, that act cannot become effective until it has been referred to the voters and has won their approval. Certain types of measures may not be subjected to a referendum. These include acts calling elections, revenue and appropriation bills, and emergency measures passed by a two-thirds vote of the legislature.

Citizens opposed to a prospective statute usually petition for a referendum only after failing to defeat the bill in the legislature and failing to get the governor to veto it. From 1911 to 1971, of the thirty-five measures subjected to referendum, twenty-one were defeated by the voters.

Direct legislation appraised

Both the initiative and referendum were subjects of considerable controversy at the time they were first proposed, and even today opinions differ widely concerning their relative advantages and disadvantages.

Opponents argue that direct legislation subverts representative government because most voters simply do not have sufficient interest or information to act intelligently on complicated legislative proposals. They claim that the legislative process is superior to plebiscitory decision making for two reasons: (1) because the former permits compromises after a measure has been drafted while the latter does not and (2) because legislators typically consider the intensity with which various views are advanced whereas in a referendum each voter's view, however keen or casual, counts the same.

Critics also fear that direct legislation opens the door for the enactment of radical and impractical legislation. Some initiative proposals have admittedly been so long and technical that only a minority of the electorate have fully understood their practical implications. Perhaps the best recent example is the 1956 oil and gas proposition, which covered thirty pages in the voters' pamphlet. It is also true that many unrealistic and unsound propositions have over the years been placed on the ballot, such as antivivisection acts, a measure to license naturopaths, single-tax proposals, and unsound pension plans. In 1964, two propositions—the constitutional amendment on open housing and a statutory initiative prohibiting pay television—were approved by the voters only to be declared invalid by the state supreme court as conflicting with certain provisions of the United States Constitution.

Another criticism often heard of the initiative and referendum is that they add unduly to the length of the ballot and consequently to the burden of the voter. That the California voter is overburdened is hardly open to question. It is not uncommon for a ballot to contain, in addition to the names of candidates for elective offices, twenty or more state propositions and several others pertaining to local issues. As shown in Table 2-1, from 1911 to 1971, a total of 665 statewide proposals were presented to the California voters. It should be noted, however that 487 of these were either constitutional amendments or other proposals submitted by the legislature. The others were submitted to

TABLE 2-1   *Statewide ballot proposals: 1911–1971*

Initiative constitutional amendments	84
Initiative legislation	59
Referendums on legislation	35
Constitutional amendments submitted by legislature	441
Bond and ballot measures submitted by legislature	46
Total	665

the voters through the initiative and referendum. Direct legislation is not, therefore, the principal reason for California's lengthy state ballots. (See Table 2-1.)

Proponents of direct legislation cite the defeat of one impractical scheme after another as proof that the electorate is capable of acting intelligently on such measures. Yet many critics believe that the rejection of such proposals is due mainly to the fact that most people apparently follow the maxim "When in doubt, vote no." They point to the record to show that more than two-thirds of all initiative measures in California have been voted down, including many that have been in the public interest—such as fair employment practice legislation, a proposal for local liquor option, and a measure that would have set up a state housing authority. Another disadvantage of the initiative is the tremendous amount of time and money needed to defeat impractical plans. For example, after defeating single-tax plans in four successive general elections, the voters in California were confronted sixteen years later with a fifth single-tax plan, which, too, was rejected.

ORIGINAL PURPOSE: TO REDUCE PRESSURE-GROUP INFLUENCE   Early proponents of the initiative and referendum believed that these government devices would enable the people to exercise more control over the legislative process and that the influence of political-interest or pressure groups would be greatly reduced. The initiative has been used to enact a number of constructive measures. These include the executive budget, the civil service system, the method of selecting judges of the state supreme court and the district courts of appeals, the permanent registration system, and the repeal of the poll tax. Supporters of direct legislation have also argued that because the initiative is available, the legislature has been stimulated to enacting measures that would otherwise

MEASURES SUBMITTED TO VOTE OF THE VOTERS

11 **BOXING AND WRESTLING CONTESTS.** Amendment of Initiative. Submitted by Legislature. Provides Legislature may amend, revise, or supplement boxing and wrestling initiative act of November 4, 1924.

YES

NO

12 **COUNTY ASSESSMENT APPEALS BOARDS.** Legislative Constitutional Amendment. Authorizes any county to create assessment appeals board to act as board of equalization of taxable property in the county.

YES

NO

13 **PROPERTY TAX STATEMENT.** Legislative Constitutional Amendment. Removes from Constitution requirement that Legislature shall require each taxpayer file annual property statement.

YES

NO

14 **PERSONAL INCOME TAXES.** Legislative Constitutional Amendment. Authorizes Legislature to provide for reporting and collecting California personal income taxes by reference to provisions of the laws of the United States and may prescribe exceptions and modifications thereto.

YES

NO

15 **ELIGIBILITY TO VOTE.** Legislative Constitutional Amendment. Provides that educational requirement for eligibility to vote shall not apply to any person who on June 27, 1952, was at least 50 years of age and a resident of the United States at least 20 years.

YES

NO

16 **OBSCENITY.** Initiative. Declares state policy is to prohibit obscene matter and conduct. Redefines "obscene" and "knowingly"; provides rules and procedure for prosecuting violations; jury unless waived determines amount of fine. Makes conspiracy to violate obscenity laws a felony. Authorizes seizure of obscene matter with procedure for summary determination of character. Requires vigorous enforcement and authorizes civil action to compel prosecutor to perform his duties.

YES

NO

FIGURE 2-2 *Of the sixteen statewide propositions on the ballot in 1966, one was an initiative and one a proposal by the legislature to amend a previous initiative.*

not have been adopted. Others question this and point out that the legislative record in California is no better than that of states like New York and Connecticut, where the initiative and referendum are not available.

USED PRIMARILY BY PRESSURE GROUPS Direct legislation has not broken the power of political-interest groups. Indeed, the great majority of initiative and referendum measures have originated with special-interest groups. Experience has shown that relatively few citizen groups interested in good government have the organization or funds necessary to secure the signatures required to place a proposition on the ballot and to conduct a successful campaign for its adoption.

As the population of the state increases, the task of securing the required number of petition signatures consequently grows. After the 1910 election, 30,853 signatures were sufficient to qualify an initiative petition. Since the 1970 election, more than 520,000 signatures are required to qualify a constitutional initiative, and more than 325,000 signatures are necessary to place a statutory initiative or referendum measure on the ballot. As the signatures must be secured within a ninety-day period, a group wishing to employ the initiative or referendum must have either a large organization or the funds necessary to pay to have the petition circulated by one of the commercial firms in San Francisco or Los Angeles which will circulate petitions at a given fee for each name obtained.[2] Along with other prices, the fees charged by "petition pushers" have risen, and the current charge for qualifying a measure for the ballot has risen to about $250,000. As many special-interest groups do have the necessary money or workers, the initiative and referendum, which were originally intended to curb the influence of pressure groups, have been used primarily by pressure groups. In the words of an as-

[2] One firm, Joseph Robinson of San Francisco, has circulated considerably more petitions than any other organization in California. On one occasion, this firm circulated petitions for opposing propositions, both of which were placed on the ballot.

"Need a Guide?" (Reprinted with permission of the San Francisco Chronicle)

semblyman: "It is now possible for any group to qualify and place on the ballot any measure they wish, no matter how outlandish, if they are able to spend $250,000 to $300,000."

COST OF PROPOSITION CAMPAIGNS The total amount spent on a proposition apparently depends largely on the amount of opposition it provokes and on the financial resources of its advocates and opponents. Although state law requires that any person or group that spends more than $1,000 on a statewide measure must file a report with the secretary of state, all expenditures on a proposition are seldom acknowledged. Even so, in a number of instances, reports listing expenses of more than half a million dollars have been filed. In 1956, nearly 5 million dollars was reported as being spent by the petroleum industry on the oil and gas initiative measure. The supporters of the proposition, the so-called big producers, paid out more than $3,420,000; the independent oil producers poured more than $1,420,000 into their successful campaign to defeat the proposal. This, incidentally, is one of the few instances in which the side spending the most money has not won.

Suggestions for reform of initiative process

With the cost of campaigning increasing, only large and well-financed special-interest groups are able to resort to the initiative process. A number of suggestions have accordingly been made concerning reforms. These include prohibiting the use of paid petition circulators;[3] restricting the process to statutory initiatives; permitting the legislature, by a two-thirds vote, to amend or repeal an initiative statute without a vote of the electorate; and making initiatives possible only by a majority vote of all those voting in the election at which the proposition is submitted, rather than by a majority of those voting on the specific measure. Several states having the initiative have adopted provisions of this type, and many students of California government would agree that their adoption in this state would be in the public interest.

[3] In 1965, Governor Edmund G. "Pat" Brown in his annual message to the legislature made the following comments regarding the initiative: "In recent years, it has often been used to turn the ballot into a field for jousting among public relations men wearing the colors of special interest. . . . I believe legislation is needed to prevent special interests from turning the initiative to private gain through the use of professional petition circulators and large sums of money."

CHAPTER 3

ℭHE ELECTORAL PROCESS

From the beginning of organized society, no problem has been more crucial and persistent than that of selecting those individuals who are to be vested with political authority. In monarchies, the ruler customarily inherits his position and is succeeded at his death by a royal prince. In dictatorships, those in control of the government ordinarily seize power and can be replaced only by superior force. In democracies, the question of who shall exercise political authority is resolved by the electoral process. The theme of this chapter is how the people of California choose their political officials; and the analysis will cover nominations, election campaigns, campaign finance, the suffrage, election practices, and the recall.

NOMINATIONS

The first step in the electoral process is the nomination of candidates for political offices. In California, parties first made nominations by conventions; but gradually the convention system fell into disrepute, due primarily to charges that the nominations were controlled by party bosses. In 1909, following the adoption of the constitutional amendment authorizing the direct primary, the California Legislature enacted a statute requiring that nominations for state offices be made by that method.

From the standpoint of procedure, the direct primary is an election closely resembling the general election. However, the purposes of the primary and of the general election are different: the primary is *to nominate candidates*; the general election is *to elect public officials.*

The party primary

Party primaries may be classified as *open* or *closed.* In an open primary, a voter is not required to declare his party affiliation and may vote the ballot of either party. In a closed primary, he is permitted to vote only for persons seeking nominations of his own party. California and the great majority of states employ the closed primary. Thus when a California voter goes to the polls in a primary election, he is handed only the ballot of the party in which he is registered. A person who registers as "declining to state" a party affiliation may not vote to nominate candidates of any party but may vote only for persons seeking nomination for nonpartisan offices.

To be a candidate in a party primary, a person must have been a registered member of that party for at least three months and must not have been a member of any other party during the year previous to filing for the nomination. Any person who can meet this requirement and who has the legal qualifications for a given office may have his name placed on his party's primary ballot by paying a small fee, filing a declaration of his candidacy, and presenting a petition signed by the required number of voters—twenty to a hundred, depending on the office—who are registered as members of that party.

A majority of California's assembly, state senate, and congressional districts may be classified as safe for one party or the other.[1] Hence, in each of these districts the party primary is the crucial contest, with the candidate of the larger party being virtually assured of victory in the general election. It is therefore especially important that all qualified persons be permitted an opportunity to seek their party's nomination in the primary election.

Nonpartisan nominations

The nonpartisan primary is employed to nominate judges, school officials, and county and municipal officers. The procedure for becoming a candidate for a nonpartisan office is similar to that followed for other elective offices in partisan primaries. The prospective nominee submits his candidacy papers and pays the filing fee, if any. His name then appears on the ballot with no party designation. Nominations for county offices and for state judicial positions are made on the first Tuesday after the first Monday in June, at the same time as nominations for state and national partisan offices.

Nonpartisan primaries are fundamentally different from party primaries. In effect a nonpartisan primary is the first stage of an election; if any person receives more than 50 percent of the votes cast for an office, he is declared the winner without his running in the general election. If no candidate receives a majority, the two with the most votes become the nominees and their names appear on the ballot in the November general election.

Most cities in California use nonpartisan elections without a primary: names of candidates are placed on the ballot by petition, and the candidate receiving a plurality of votes is elected, even though he might not have a majority. General-law cities and most charter cities hold their elections on the second Tuesday in April, although charter cities may select a different date.

In recent years, some individuals have urged the abolition of nonpartisan primaries and the nomination of all officials, except possibly judges, on a partisan basis. Others, including several state legislators,

---

[1] For instance, in the 1968 election in California only four of the thirty-eight contests for congressional seats, and ten of the eighty assembly races were won with less than 55 per cent of the votes; of the twenty elections for state senate seats only four victorious candidates received less than 60 per cent of the votes.

THE GOVERNMENT AND POLITICS OF CALIFORNIA

would like to see elections for the legislature placed on a nonpartisan basis. A study of nonpartisan elections in California indicates that more Republicans than Democrats have been elected to nonpartisan offices. For example, in 1955 in twenty-six cities with more than 50,000 population, 68 percent of the council members and 80 percent of the mayors were registered Republicans.[2] Although most local elections in California continue to be strictly nonpartisan, in recent years more efforts have been made by members of both parties to secure the election of members of their party to local offices.

The presidential primary

In California, the voter is permitted to express a preference among aspirants for his party's nomination for President and, at the same time, vote for delegates to its national convention.[3] Delegates are selected, however, as a group, not individually. The names of the prospective delegates do not appear on the ballot, only the names of the candidates to whom the slates of delegates are pledged. The names comprising each slate are printed separately and mailed with the sample ballot to each voter. Members of such a delegation are pledged to vote for their candidate for the presidency until released by the chairman of the delegation. It is also possible for an unpledged delegation to be selected to attend the national convention. In 1968, a slate of delegates pledged to Senator Robert F. Kennedy won the Democratic presidential primary; however, after Kennedy's tragic assassination on the evening of his victory, the delegates could then vote for any other candidate.

Any three or more registered members of a party may form a committee to organize a slate of delegates. If a slate is pledged to support a particular candidate, his written consent must be obtained. At least two members of the delegation must be chosen from each congressional district to make sure that each section of the state will be represented. Usually, delegates are party leaders in their own districts and pay their own convention expenses. The California presidential pri-

---

[2] Eugene C. Lee, *The Politics of Nonpartisanship*, Berkeley: University of California Press, 1960, pp. 56–57.
[3] Fewer than one-third of the states use some type of presidential primary. Most of the other states select delegates to the national conventions by state or district conventions, although a few states permit committees to choose the delegates.

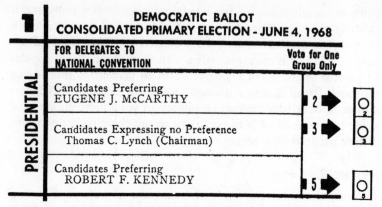

DEMOCRATIC BALLOT
CONSOLIDATED PRIMARY ELECTION - JUNE 4, 1968

1

PRESIDENTIAL

FOR DELEGATES TO NATIONAL CONVENTION	Vote for One Group Only
Candidates Preferring EUGENE J. McCARTHY	2 ➡ ⊘₂
Candidates Expressing no Preference Thomas C. Lynch (Chairman)	3 ➡ ⊘₃
Candidates Preferring ROBERT F. KENNEDY	5 ➡ ⊘₅

FIGURE 3-1 *In the presidential primary the voter, by indicating his choice among the names on the ballot, votes for a slate to attend the national convention. A slate is identified by the candidate to whom it is pledged, or if a slate is uninstructed, by its chairman*

mary is held in conjunction with the regular party primary in June, immediately preceding the quadrennial national party conventions.[4]

CAMPAIGNS

Many kinds of political campaigns are waged in California. They range from the colorful, highly organized contests directed toward electing a President, governor, or United States senator or securing adoption of a controversial ballot proposition to the less interesting and unprofessional, although not unimportant, struggles for local offices. It is sometimes difficult to determine exactly when a campaign begins and ends, for many prospective candidates start preparing for entry into public life months before they file for office; and most public officials throughout their terms in office continue to campaign in order to win votes in the succeeding election. When we discuss political campaigns, however,

[4] In 1968 and 1969, the legislature passed a measure, vetoed each time by Governor Reagan, which was patterned on the Oregon presidential primary and provided for the secretary of state to place on the primary ballot the names of all nationally recognized presidential contenders.

we generally refer to the political activities of the period immediately preceding a primary or general election during which concerted efforts are made to gain electoral support.

Campaign organizations and strategy

Research on electoral behavior in the United States indicates that individual voting decisions are usually based on the voters' perception of the parties, the candidates, and the issues. The tradition of voter independence and loose partisan ties have caused most California candidates to conduct personal, nonpartisan campaigns aimed principally at publicizing themselves and winning votes from members of both parties. Although parties have been stronger and more active in political campaigns since the early 1960s than formerly, candidates customarily rely relatively little upon their party organizations, creating instead campaign organizations composed primarily of personal friends and supporters. Members of party central committees often serve on campaign committees of candidates, but these tend to be personal rather than party organizations. Candidates with constituencies composed of the entire state usually form separate campaign organizations for northern and southern California, each functioning independently of the other, with separate managers, finance committees, and local chairmen and committees set up in the counties and cities. Campaign managers and local chairmen are often selected because of their prestige, while the actual direction of the campaign is placed in the hands of paid professional staff members or a campaign management firm.

Nominees for statewide offices such as governor or United States senator commonly appeal to members of the opposing party by creating committees composed of registered voters of that party who are pledged to support their candidacy. Thus during campaigns there are committees of Democrats urging the electorate to support Republican candidates and committees of Republicans endorsing Democratic candidates.

The decision whether to wage a partisan or a nonpartisan type of campaign will naturally be based on which will apparently produce more votes for the individual candidate. Realistic appraisal of the political situation in California at the present time apparently leads most nominees of the Republican party and well-known candidates of the Democratic party to favor nonpartisan campaigns, but less well-known candidates of the Democratic party evidently believe that they have more to gain by making an appeal for partisan support. For example, in 1966 and 1970, Ronald Reagan stated on several occasions: "I don't see any issues that don't cut across party lines." Edmund G. "Pat" Brown, the Democratic nominee for governor in 1958, 1962, and 1966, conducted highly nonpartisan campaigns, but most other Democratic candidates, hoping to benefit from the fact that there were a million more registered Democrats than Republicans in the state, tended to place more stress on their partisan affiliation.

Candidates make herculean efforts to meet and talk to as many voters as possible. They deliver addresses at public rallies, at meetings of organized groups and clubs, at factories during lunch hours, and on other occasions. Coffee hours and cocktail parties, enabling nominees to meet smaller groups, are held in homes, and often candidates tour their constituencies, talking and shaking hands with as many people as is physically possible. For example, when Richard M. Nixon ran for governor in 1962, his campaign manager announced that he had traveled 17,775 miles, seen 445,800 Californians, and shaken 163,000 hands. But because of the millions of California voters and the miles to be traveled to reach them, most candidates for statewide office must rely to a large extent on the media of mass communication.

PROFESSIONAL CAMPAIGN MANAGERS Because of several factors—principally the desire of candidates to make the most effective use of the mass media and the lack of strong parties with permanent and active organizations at the precinct level—candidates use public relations and advertising firms more extensively in California than in any other state. One party leader, in explaining the widespread employment of professional campaign management firms, commented: "Politics has become too expensive and too complicated to leave to amateurs."

The use of these opinion-management experts, or "image makers," varies considerably. Candidates for lesser offices may not have sufficient funds or deem it necessary to employ professional public relations personnel. In some statewide contests professional campaign-management firms are not used, and advertising personnel are used primarily as technicians, only to arrange for space in the press and for time on radio and television. But in a number of instances firms have been employed to take virtually complete charge of a campaign. For a sizable fee these organizations will undertake to sell a candidate or a ballot measure to the voters in much the same fashion as advertising agencies sell soap, cereal, or automobiles.[5] These public relations firms will plan the overall campaign strategy, raise funds, prepare the candidate's speeches and campaign literature, handle press releases, make all arrangements for the candidate's public appearances, and prepare the advertising copy or film used in the press and on radio or television. In his 1966 and 1970 gubernatorial campaigns Ronald Reagan employed the firm of Spencer-Roberts and Associates, which reportedly was given broad responsibilities in his campaign.[6]

Campaigns and the mass media

Candidates and campaign managers seek the support of the press, for they find that if a newspaper endorses a candidate it often will aid him in its news columns as well as on its editorial pages. A recent study of the California press indicates that although newspaper support is influential in most campaigns it tends to be more significant in local elections, on ballot propositions, and in races for the legislature than in statewide elections.[7]

Candidates for major offices budget large amounts for radio and television time, advertising in the press, billboards, leaflets and pamphlets, posters, bumper strips, and other items. Practical politicians and

---

[5] During the 1964 senatorial campaign, an official of the firm handling television bookings for Pierre Salinger remarked, "as far as I am concerned, Pierre Salinger is a bar of soap and we're going to sell him as effectively as we can." John R. Owens, *Money and Politics in California: Democratic Senatorial Primary, 1964,* Princeton, N. J.: Citizens' Research Foundation, 1966, p. 43.

[6] One of the partners of the firm explained the approach of their organization: "As far as overall direction is concerned we control where the candidate goes, the schedule, the organization, and the timing—when you move on different issues." Walt Anderson, "Spencer-Roberts: Dynamic Duo of California Politics," *Los Angeles Times West Magazine,* Dec. 11, 1966, p. 27. Spencer-Roberts reportedly received a fee, above expenses, of approximately $150,000 for directing Reagan's 1966 campaign. Jack Langguth, "Political Fun and Games in California," *The New York Times Magazine,* Oct. 16, 1966, p. 156.

[7] James E. Gregg, *Newspaper Editorial Endorsements: Their Influence on California Elections, 1948-1962,* unpublished doctoral dissertation, University of California, Santa Barbara, 1964.

"Well, I made up my mind—I'm going to vote for the guy who couldn't afford paid political announcements!" (Copyright Los Angeles Times, reprinted with its permission)

public relations experts agree that of the various channels of mass communication, television is the most effective, for face-to-face contact between the candidate and the voter is more closely approximated on television than through any other mass medium. In recent years, candidates have attempted to make maximum use of television by delivering addresses, appearing on televised press conferences, scheduling question-and-answer programs, and preparing spots—short films that can be shown between regular programs.

Television was undoubtedly used more in the 1966 and 1970 campaigns than in any previous election years in California. In each year, Reagan announced his candidacy with a prerecorded television and radio broadcast on stations covering the state. Most candidates for major offices made extensive use of previously filmed "spots" or short—one to five minute—programs that oversimplified the issues.

Every political candidate is confronted with the problem of voter apathy. The head of one public relations firm has expressed the opinion that the only way to attract the attention of the voters is to give them "a show or a fight." Both tactics are employed. To entertain the voters, motion picture and television stars are used extensively in campaigns.

"Personality Politics"

As in many other states, election campaigns in California tend to emphasize personalities more than issues. Virtually without exception, a nominee is portrayed as an upright, intelligent, courageous citizen of highest integrity and honesty, who can always be trusted to act in the interest of the general public. If the aspirant for office has an attractive wife and children, so much the better; their pictures will be displayed prominently in his campaign literature to help convey to the electorate the desired image of the candidate. By making extensive use of the candidate's picture on billboards and posters and in the press and by arranging television advertisements and appearances, campaign managers attempt to transform their candidate into a celebrity—in much the same way that motion picture and television stars become celebrities.

Movie and television actors have long been used by candidates as drawing cards in their campaigns, but only in recent years have movie stars themselves run for political office. The most notable examples are Ronald Reagan, George Murphy, and Shirley Temple Black. Such candidates are "pre-sold" public figures and have advantages over other political novices. Individuals are attracted to their candidacy not because of their knowledge, leadership ability, or political experience but because of their pleasant personalities and what has been referred to as the "curious magnetism of stardom."

Although election campaigns tend to be based more on personalities than on current issues, most candidates do, of course, discuss a variety of issues and problems. In recent elections, some candidates have conducted public opinion surveys to help determine which issues to stress in their campaigns.

Smear tactics

As candidates tend to focus their campaigns on their personal qualifications, it is not surprising that questions are raised by their opponents regarding those personal attributes. Occasionally, statements and tactics go beyond the bounds of fair play, and attempts are made to win elections by smearing the opponent. Some liberal candidates have been charged with Communist or radical connections and even encouraging riots, disloyalty to America, and anarchy. On the other hand, conservative candidates have been depicted as reactionaries who, if elected, would use their office solely to aid the vested business interests. On occasion, candidates and their families have become targets of mud-slinging campaigns characterized by false and malicious rumors and accusations. Another deplorable practice in recent years has been the effort to disrupt meetings and to prevent persons from delivering public addresses by taunts, demonstrations, and other calculated disturbances. Such practices, virtually unknown in California until the late 1960s, undermine the democratic process.

Group appeals

Experienced politicians and professional public relations personnel are aware that the voting behavior of the average citizen is influenced by a variety of factors, one of which is his membership in organized groups. For this reason, candidates attempt to win the support of as many different groups as possible. In many instances nominees seek the outright endorsement of an organization. In order to appeal for the backing of major groups, candidates often organize committees headed by prominent members of business, labor, agricultural, professional, and veterans' groups in order to elicit the votes of rank-and-file members.

Certain political-interest groups have at times actively assisted candidates seeking election. Some groups have lent their lobbyists or political counsels to candidates to advise them on planning and executing their campaign strategy. Organized groups also have often provided candidates with campaign funds and workers. According to reports, old-age-pension groups, organized labor, and several business groups have in some instances taken almost complete responsibility for directing campaigns.

CAMPAIGN FINANCE

Financing campaigns has long been a major problem in democratic politics. A great deal of money is required to conduct an effective campaign, yet no completely satisfactory means have been found for raising such funds. During recent years, campaign costs in California have risen sharply, due largely to the general increase in prices, the growth in population, and the increased use of the mass media. As the costs of campaigns mount, the problems revolving around political contributions and expenditures become ever more acute.

There is no question but that a considerable amount of money is required to elect a candidate to most partisan offices in California and that a certain minimum amount is necessary in order to make the race. It is therefore obvious that those who control the major contributions may determine who can and cannot run for a particular office. Within both parties, examples can be found of prospective candidates for a particular office who failed to run because they learned that sufficient funds would not be forthcoming.

The candidate who spends the most money usually wins; but this does not necessarily indicate that the outcome of an election depends principally on campaign funds. The candidate most likely to win is often able to elicit more funds and other types of support than his opponent, primarily because individuals and groups like to support a winner. Moreover, it is not uncommon for a successful candidate to have less funds than his opponent. The lack of money may be offset by an effective campaign and by enthusiastic volunteer workers. The chief purpose of campaign funds is to enable the candidate to gain access to the electorate with his appeal for votes, and beyond a certain point, additional financial support may make little difference in the outcome of an election.

What campaigns cost

For a variety of reasons it is impossible to determine the exact cost of a given campaign: (1) As will be explained, reports of campaign expenditures are seldom complete or entirely accurate; (2) expenditures that aid all the candidates running on a party ticket are usually not attributed to the individual candidates; (3) certain individuals and organizations subsidize some candidates' campaigns by making available without charge such items as office space and equipment, billboards, and workers from their staffs or by placing employees of the candidate on the company's payrolls. These contributions, which represent expenditures, do not show up on campaign reports.

Although the candidates' reports do not show the exact amount spent, they give some indication of the high costs of conducting campaigns. In 1968, the Kennedy and McCarthy forces together spent an estimated 3.5 million dollars in the presidential primary in California. As would be expected, it costs more to run for governor than for any other state office. The reported campaign expenditures of candidates for this position in 1966 and 1970 were higher than in any previous election (see Table 3-1).

TABLE 3-1   *1966 and 1970 gubernatorial campaign expenditures*

Year	Candidate	Primary	General election	Total
1966	Brown	$561,876	$2,115,966	$2,677,842
	Reagan	544,200	3,259,346	3,803,546
1970	Reagan	860,179	2,135,981	2,996,160
	Unruh	320,042	887,822	1,207,864

In 1968, a total of more than $4,450,000 was reported as being spent in the United States senatorial race by Alan Cranston, Thomas Kuchel, and Max Rafferty. Campaigns for other statewide offices often are quite expensive. Individual aspirants for such state executive offices as attorney general and secretary of state have reported expenditures as low as $40,000 and as high as $350,000.

Running for other offices in California also costs a considerable amount. According to estimates based on previous campaigns, a mayoralty candidate in Los Angeles or San Francisco should expect to spend from $300,000 to more than $1,000,000.[8] The expense of running for the state senate and assembly varies greatly. If only token opposition exists, a candidate for the legislature may spend as little as $2,000 or $3,000, but where strong opposition is encountered, expenditures of more than $100,000 have been reported.

How money is spent

A brief look at the purposes for which money is spent helps to explain why campaigns cost so much. The amount spent and the purposes for which it is spent will, of course, vary according to the office sought, the candidate, and the funds available. But most campaign expenditures may be grouped in one of four categories.

1. *Publicity expenses.* These expenditures, which include fees paid public relations or advertising personnel, television and radio expenditures, advertising in the press, direct mailings, billboards, posters, pamphlets, bumper stickers, and other items, undoubtedly consume the largest share of the campaign dollar in California. For example, a ten-second spot at prime time on a top Los Angeles television station costs $800, and a full-page ad in a Los Angeles newspaper costs $5,000. Candidates for statewide office have devoted as much as 75 percent of their funds for publicity. In the 1968 primary and general elections in California, political parties

[8] In the Los Angeles mayoralty race in 1969, unsuccessful candidate Thomas Bradley filed reports showing expenditures of $418,750.54 in the primary elections and $627,192.27 in the general election. Sam Yorty, the incumbent mayor who was re-elected, reported expenditures of $286,316.92 in the primary and $517,450.10 in the general election.

and candidates spent more than 5 million dollars for television and radio time.[9]

2. *General overhead expenses.* Under this item are included charges for office space and the salaries paid professional campaign managers, secretaries, clerks, research workers, and other staff employees. Although many of the campaign workers are volunteers, a number of such paid workers must be employed in major campaigns.

3. *Field activities.* This item includes payments for transportation, hotel rooms, and meals. Candidates for statewide office find that these expenses may run into large amounts. For instance in Brown's 1966 campaign for governor, he reported $131,309 for travel.

4. *Election day expenses.* One of the major election day expenses is the outlay for transporting voters to the polls. After one election, the Los Angeles County Republican Central Committee reported that 2,000 cars had been mobilized for that purpose. In some areas, election day budgets may contain sums for poll watchers, messengers, and telephone committees.

Raising political funds

California's two major parties have used slightly different procedures for raising funds. The Republicans have organized and have made effective use of United Republican Finance Committees. Separate regional committees have been created in northern and southern California, and committees have also been organized on a county basis. These committees, composed, to a large extent, of well-known business and civic leaders, have organized their fund-raising drives in much the same fashion as charitable organizations. Each Republican candidate presents his campaign budget to the committees, which decide how much he may expect to receive. The candidates also make individual efforts to raise funds for their campaigns.

The Democrats have experimented with united fund drives in a few counties, but most of their campaign funds are raised by the individual candidates and temporary campaign committees. The central

[9] "Campaign Spending in the 1968 Elections," *Congressional Quarterly Weekly Report*, vol. 27, no. 49, Dec. 5, 1969, p. 2442.

committees have also created informal finance committees, often headed by wealthy individuals who have proven ability at soliciting funds.

Sources of campaign funds

Due to candidates' inadequate financial reports, it is not possible to know the exact source of campaign funds. However, available information indicates that the donors may be classified into four groups.

First, there are contributions by the candidates, their relatives, friends, and other wealthy individuals. If a candidate is wealthy or has affluent relatives or friends, a large proportion of his funds may come from these sources. In 1970 Norton Simon and his wife contributed $1.8 million of the approximately $2 million he spent in his unsuccessful effort to win the Republican nomination for the United States Senate. Most candidates for such offices as governor or United States senator customarily receive large amounts from individual contributors. For instance, among Reagan's chief financial supporters were five wealthy friends and political advisors often referred to as his "kitchen cabinet."[10]

Second, both parties solicit funds from various small contributors, the rank-and-file party members. The Democrats have organized "Dollars for Democrats" drives in which they have attempted to get volunteer party workers to make a house-to-house canvass of registered Democrats. In 1964, Barry Goldwater and, in 1966, Ronald Reagan, through television and newspaper advertising and through direct mail solicitation in California, sought numerous small contributions from supporters. Various other efforts have also been made to induce the general electorate to contribute. But public opinion polls show that no more than 10 to 12 percent of the electorate contribute to campaigns, and the total amount contributed by the small donor undoubtedly represents only a small percentage of campaign funds.

Third, each party and some leading candidates derive a large amount of money from fund-raising activities. Both parties organize fund-raising dinners, barbecues, and other benefit functions, with indi-

---

[10] These men are Leonard Firestone, tire company executive; Henry Salvatori, oil company officer; Holmes Tuttle, auto dealer; Jaquelin Hume, food company executive; and Taft Schreiber, Reagan's agent when he was in motion pictures. *Los Angeles Times*, May 14, 1970.

vidual tickets usually selling at $10 to $100. In recent years the parties and individual candidates have had a number of dinners at which as much as $400,000 has been raised. Included among fund-raising activities is the sale of advertising to corporations and other firms in political programs and books.

Fourth, a major source of political funds in California is the organized interest group. For instance, many of the tickets to fund-raising activities are purchased by members of such groups. In addition, some groups contribute indirectly through their officers or their lobbyists. The names of several lobbyists appear with surprising frequency on the campaign reports of members of the state legislature, and, as might be expected, some lobbyists contribute to the campaigns of both Democrats and Republicans. A technique employed in the 1970 campaign by several California public utility companies was for the executives of a firm such as General Telephone or Pacific Gas and Electric to form a "good government club" and collect funds which were then contributed to candidates. According to one utility official, the funds were given to candidates "who recognize the need for the industry and who will effectively represent us." Many candidates accept campaign contributions without becoming beholden to the donors. But, in the words of one state senator: "Every candidate, unless he is personally wealthy, must approach special-interest groups to aid him in financing his campaign. Naturally, donations from such groups seldom come with no strings attached."

Regulation of campaign finance

PRESENT LAW   California's regulation of campaign finance (corrupt practices legislation) was changed in 1969 to require more adequate reporting of contributions to political campaigns. Presently, candidates and campaign committees must file reports listing the names of donors contributing more than $500 and the amount of each such contribution, the names only of all donors contributing less than $500, the total amount received by each candidate, the purposes for which all expenditures were made, and the names of all persons to whom money was paid, lent, or given.

The term "contributions" is defined in the law to include gifts, loans, subscriptions, deposits of money, or "anything of value," including "the services of an employee donated by an employer." Candidates and campaign committees must file reports with the secretary of state and the clerk of the county in which they reside twenty to twenty-five days before and thirty to thirty-five days after primary and general elections.

REFORMS SUGGESTED   There is widespread agreement among students of California politics that new legislation is badly needed. Proposals for such legislation fall into two general categories: suggestions for assisting candidates and parties to meet legitimate campaign expenses, and proposals for additional regulation.

Of the proposals for aiding candidates, three merit serious consideration. (1) Each serious candidate might have a certain amount of time on television and radio made available to him without charge. (2) Each candidate for partisan office might be permitted to have, in the handbook which is distributed to the voters before elections, a page to describe his qualifications for office. (3) A concerted effort should be made, through public service advertising, tax exemption, or other means, to induce rank-and-file voters to contribute small amounts to the party or candidates whom they favor. The California Legislature has taken a step in this direction by providing that each individual might deduct campaign contributions not in excess of $100 from his state income tax.

The experience of states that have recently enacted new corrupt practices legislation indicates that such a new statute in California should incorporate the following provisions for improving the regulation of campaign finance:

1. *Centralized responsibility.* Each candidate should be required to appoint a treasurer. All contributions should be channeled through the treasurer, and no expenditures should be permitted on behalf of a candidate unless authorized by this agent. All funds should be deposited in a bank within a specified time and receipts should be kept for all expenditures.
2. *Limitation on contributions.* No individual should be permitted to contribute more than a specified amount—possibly $1,000—to any

one candidate or campaign committee. Such a limitation would prevent a candidate from becoming unduly obligated to any person or group due to campaign contributions.

3. *Groups prohibited from contributing.* The federal government and some states prohibit corporations, labor unions, persons with government contracts, and certain other groups from making campaign contributions. A provision of this type would be desirable in California.

4. *Enforcement of the act.* Some official or government agency should be charged with strictly enforcing the regulations, in particular insuring that all candidates and campaign committees file reports and that these reports are accurate. Moreover, provision should be made for publicizing the information in the reports.

Bills introduced in each of the recent sessions of the California Legislature have included all or most of these provisions, but they have not been adopted. The enactment of a statute including these provisions would certainly have a healthy, democratizing effect on California politics.

ELECTORAL BEHAVIOR

Voter qualifications

In California, a voter must be a citizen of the United States, twenty-one years of age, able to read the state constitution in English or Spanish,[11] and able to sign his name. Voters must also register and meet a residential requirement which consists of residing in the state for a year, in the county for ninety days, and in the precinct for fifty-four days. A person may vote in a presidential election without meeting the usual residence requirements after residing in the state for fifty-four

[11] Formerly the state constitution required voters to be able to read English. However, in 1970 the California Supreme Court ruled that this provision was a violation of the equal protection clause of the Fourteenth Amendment of the United States Constitution and that non-English-speaking persons with access to political information in their own language are entitled to vote. This decision has been interpreted as enfranchising all Spanish-speaking citizens.

days if he meets all other California qualifications and was a qualified voter in the state of his previous residence.[12]

Two general types of registration systems, permanent and periodic, are used by the various states. California and all but twelve other states employ permanent registration.[13] Once a person is registered, he need not register again unless since last registering he has moved, has changed his name, wishes to change his party affiliation, or failed to vote in the preceding general election. If a person fails to vote, he is mailed a double postcard, one part of which informs him that his registration is cancelled unless he returns the second part of the card, which states that he has not changed his address.

Undoubtedly, the percentage of Californians voting would be increased if voting requirements were less difficult. Suggested changes in requirements include reducing the residency requirements to six months in the state and thirty days in the precinct and county and changing the cutoff date for registration so that persons could register any time up to one or two weeks prior to the election.

Voter turnout

A smaller proportion of persons of voting age go to the polls on election day in California than in most other Northern states. In the nine presidential elections from 1936 through 1968, an average of 64 percent of Californians twenty-one years and over voted, ranking California thirtieth among the states in voter turnout. Of the states with poorer voting records, approximately two-thirds were Southern or border

[12] In 1970 Congress passed a measure providing for: A minimum voting age of eighteen for all federal, state, and local elections, starting January 1, 1971; the suspension of any literacy test for five years; and a uniform residence requirement of only thirty days to qualify a person to vote in presidential elections. In December, 1970, the United States Supreme Court upheld the constitutionality of all of these provisions except the minimum voting age of eighteen in state elections; California state legislators then announced plans for amending the state constitution to establish this provision.

[13] The purpose of registration is to provide the precinct election boards with lists of qualified voters. A person may register in the office of the county clerk. Registration tables may also be set upon the city streets or elsewhere and manned by deputy registrars who are paid nominal fees for each person they register.

states.[14] In mid-term elections during the past two decades, California has ranked twentieth, about half of the states with lower voting percentages being Southern or border states. California's higher ranking in mid-term than in general elections may be explained primarily by the fact that the governor and the other state elective executives are chosen in mid-term elections in California but not in all other states.

One reason for nonvoting is the failure of people to register. During the two decades from 1950 to 1970, at the time of each election 20 to 30 percent of Californians of voting age had not registered and therefore could not vote. For instance, in the 1968 general election 27 percent, or nearly 3 million Californians twenty-one or older had not registered. Of those registered, 10 to 15 percent fail to vote in a presidential election year and 20 to 30 percent in the off-year elections. Various reasons may, of course, be cited to explain why people do not vote, including illness, lack of interest, or being away from home and failing to obtain an absentee ballot.

Voting patterns

In most respects, the California electorate is representative of American voters in general. Since the 1930s, there have been more Democrats than Republicans nationally, and in California the former have outnumbered the latter by approximately a 4 to 3 ratio (see Figure 3-1). For instance, in 1968, registered voters in California were divided as follows: 54.5 percent Democrats, 40.3 percent Republicans, 1.1 percent American Independent, and 0.7 percent Peace and Freedom; 3.3 per cent "declined to state." As will be explained in the following chapter, the Republicans have been more successful in electing California officials than in controlling the presidency or Congress.

In terms of socioeconomic characteristics, Democratic and Republican voters in California are similar to their counterparts across the country. Public opinion surveys show that each of the major parties draws members from every major segment of the population, but not in the same proportion. In brief, in comparison with the Democrats, the Republicans generally receive more support from upper-income groups,

[14] Edmond Costantini and Willis D. Hawley, "Increasing Participation in California Elections: The Need for Electoral Reform," *Public Affairs Report*, vol. 10, no. 3, June, 1969.

businessmen, professional people other than those in education, those with college educations, older people, Protestants, and people who live in suburbs and small towns and on farms. More Democrats than Republicans are in low-income categories, are members of labor unions and of racial or religious minorities, live in large cities, are under forty years of age, and have only elementary or high school educations.

Certain groups of Democrats—in particular those with low incomes and some ethnic minorities, in comparison to other socioeconomic groupings—are less likely to register and, if registered, are less likely to vote. Moreover, California Democrats apparently are more willing to split their ballots and vote for candidates of the opposite party than are the Republicans. Because of these voting tendencies, Democratic candidates for statewide offices seldom poll as many votes as the Democratic percentage of the two-party registration; on the other hand, Republican candidates consistently receive a larger share of the vote than their proportion of the registered voters (see Table 3-2). Indeed, it is not uncommon for Republican candidates to receive more votes than the total number of Republican registrants.[15] As will be dis-

[15] For example, in 1968 in California Richard M. Nixon received 3,467,664 votes for President, 5,533 more than the 3,462,131 registered Republicans. There were 4,682,661 registered Democrats but Democratic candidate Hubert H. Humphrey received only 3,244,318 votes.

TABLE 3-2 *Democratic percentage of two-party registration and vote for major offices, 1956–1970*

Year	Registration	Vote for				
		PRESIDENT	GOVERNOR	U.S. SENATE	CONGRESS	ASSEMBLY
1956	57.4	44.4		45.8	52.4	53.4
1958	59.2		59.8	57.1	60.0	58.9
1960	59.5	49.7			53.9	54.0
1962	58.8		52.6	43.5	51.8	53.9
1964	59.8	59.2		48.5	52.9	53.6
1966	58.5		42.3		46.8	46.3
1968	57.5	48.6		52.6	44.8	45.9
1970	57.9		45.5	54.7	50.1	50.7

SOURCE: Adapted from Totton J. Anderson and Eugene C. Lee, "The 1966 Election in California," *Western Political Quarterly*, vol. 20, no. 2, pt. 2, pp. 535–554, June, 1967.

cussed in the following chapter, these voting patterns help to explain why the Republicans often win elections, although they have fewer party identifiers than the Democrats.

Election returns indicate different voting patterns in northern and southern California. Traditionally, the state has been divided into north and south sections by the Tehachapi Mountains. Northern Californians tend to register in larger proportions as Democrats and to support liberal programs. Democratic candidates for statewide offices receive their strongest support in the urban San Francisco Bay counties and from the Central Valley counties of Sacramento, Fresno, Madera, and Merced. Voters in the eight southern counties generally are more likely to be Republicans and more conservative. Republican candidates for major offices can expect to receive sizable majorities in Orange, San Diego, and Riverside Counties; thus they may lose the northern counties by as much as 200,000 votes and be elected because of the heavy Republican vote in the southern part of the state. For instance, in 1960 and 1968, Richard Nixon in his bid for the Presidency failed to carry northern California but won the state's electoral votes because of the southern counties. In 1968, southern California gave Nixon a 394,000 margin, of which 270,000 came from Orange and San Diego counties, but because he was outpolled in northern California his statewide victory vote edge was only 223,000.

ELECTIONS

Types of elections

As in other states, various types of elections are held in California. They may be classified into five groups. (1) Primary elections to nominate candidates for office are held in June prior to the general elections. (2) General elections are held on the first Tuesday after the first Monday in November of each even-numbered year. (3) Municipal elections are held in general-law cities on the second Tuesday in April of each odd-numbered year and in other cities on the dates prescribed by the city charters. (4) Special elections may be called by county boards of supervisors and city councils within their jurisdictions; the governor may also call special elections to fill vacancies in state elective offices and to allow the electorate to vote on initiative, referendum, and recall proposals. (5) Numerous local elections are held at various times for the purpose of electing officials to school boards and other special district boards and for the purpose of voting on proposals affecting these districts.

Conducting the elections

The secretary of state is California's principal election officer. His responsibilities relating to elections include preparing the ballot, canvassing the returns and certifying the nomination and election of candidates for state offices, and serving as the custodian for reports of campaign expenditures. The actual conducting of elections is primarily in the hands of local officials. City councils and city clerks are responsible for municipal elections. Most of the responsibility for other elections is exercised by county officials: the boards of supervisors and the county clerk, or, in the larger counties, the boards of supervisors and the registrars of voters.[16]

California uses the office-block type of ballot, with national, state, and county candidates grouped together according to the office they are seeking (see Figure 3-2). The other principal kind of ballot used by states is the party-column type, which lists the candidates in columns according to their party. Precinct election boards vary in size from three to six members, depending on the type of election and the size of the precinct. Provision is made for a recount of ballots from any precinct or precincts if any candidate or the county board believes it desirable. Approximately one-third of the counties use voting machines or ballots that are counted by electronic tabulators.

Any California voter may cast an absentee ballot if he expects to be absent from his home on election day or is physically unable to go to the polls. Absentee ballots must be returned not later than three days before an election so that they can be counted with the other ballots on election day.

---

[16] San Francisco, which is a city-county, is the only county with a separate board of election commissioners. Elections in certain special districts are administered by the officers of those districts.

(This number shall be torn off by inspector and handed to the voter)

SAMPLE BALLOT
No. 123456

112

MARK (●) BALLOT **ONLY WITH MARKING DEVICE**

(Fold ballot to this perforated line, leaving top margin exposed)

GENERAL BALLOT — 13th CONGRESSIONAL, 24th SENATORIAL, 36th ASSEMBLY DISTRICT — TUESDAY, NOVEMBER 3, 1970

INSTRUCTIONS TO VOTERS: To vote for a candidate of your selection for any office of Judge of the Supreme Court or any office of Judge of a Court of Appeal, stamp a mark (●) in the voting square after the word "YES," to the right of the name of the candidate. To vote against that candidate, stamp a mark (●) in the voting square after the word "NO," to the right of the name of that candidate. To vote for any other candidate of your selection, stamp a mark (●) in the voting square next to the right of the name of that candidate. Where two or more candidates for the same office are to be elected, stamp a mark (●) after the names of all the candidates for that office for whom you desire to vote, not to exceed, however, the number of candidates who are to be elected. To vote for a person not on the ballot, write his name under the title of the office in the blank space left for that purpose and stamp a mark (●) in the voting square next to the right of the name of that person. To vote on any measure, stamp a mark (●) in the voting square after the word "YES" or after the word "NO." All marks, except the mark (●) are forbidden. All distinguishing marks or erasures are forbidden and make the ballot void. If you wrongly stamp, tear or deface this ballot, return it to the inspector of election and obtain another.

STATE

Governor — Vote for One
- RONALD REAGAN, Republican — Governor
- JESS UNRUH, Democratic — California State Legislator
- RICARDO ROMO, Peace and Freedom — Political Organizer
- WILLIAM K. SHEARER, American Independent — Publisher

Lieutenant Governor — Vote for One
- ED REINECKE, Republican — Lieutenant Governor
- MERWYN H. HEMP, American Independent — Mathematician
- ALFRED E. ALQUIST, Democratic — California State Senator
- JOHN HAAG, Peace and Freedom — Organizer

Secretary of State — Vote for One
- THOMAS M. GOODLOE, JR., American Independent — El Dorado County Supervisor
- EDMUND G. BROWN, JR., Democratic — Attorney at Law
- ISRAEL FEUER, Peace and Freedom — Community Organizer
- JAMES L. FLOURNOY, Republican — Attorney at Law

Controller — Vote for One
- HOUSTON I. FLOURNOY, Republican — Controller, State of California
- C. T. WEBER, Peace and Freedom — Historian
- RONALD BROOKS CAMERON, Democratic — Certified Public Accountant

Treasurer — Vote for One
- IVY BAKER PRIEST, Republican — Treasurer of the State of California
- JACK HAMPTON, Peace and Freedom — Theatrical Agent
- MILTON G. GORDON, Democratic — Administrative Officer-Treasurer

Attorney General — Vote for One
- EVELLE J. YOUNGER, Republican — District Attorney
- MARGUERITE M. (MARGE) BUCKLEY, Peace and Freedom — Attorney
- CHARLES A. O'BRIEN, Democratic — Deputy Attorney General

Member, State Board of Equalization, Fourth District — Vote for One
- RICHARD NEVINS, Democratic — Member, State Board of Equalization, Fourth District
- HOWARD JARVIS, Republican — Tax Reduction Expert
- MARYLOU CUSHMAN, American Independent — Journalist

CONGRESSIONAL

United States Senator — Vote for One
- GEORGE MURPHY, Republican — United States Senator
- JOHN V. TUNNEY, Democratic — United States Congressman
- CHARLES C. RIPLEY, American Independent — Engineer
- ROBERT SCHEER, Peace and Freedom

Representative in Congress 13th District — Vote for One
- CHARLES M. TEAGUE, Republican — United States Congressman
- GARY K. HART, Democratic — Educator
- MAUDE I. JORDET, American Independent — Housewife

STATE LEGISLATURE

State Senator 24th District — Vote for One
- ROBERT J. LAGOMARSINO, Republican — State Senator, 24th Senatorial District, California Legislature
- JAMES J. COLLINS, American Independent
- RUSSELL G. HERRON, Democratic — Aerospace Environmental Physicist

Member of Assembly 36th District — Vote for One
- W. DON Mac GILLIVRAY, Republican — Incumbent Assemblyman, 36th District
- KENNETH A. PALMER, Democratic — Business, Government Consultant

SCHOOL

State Superintendent of Public Instruction — Vote for One
- MAX RAFFERTY — State Superintendent of Public Instruction
- WILSON RILES — Deputy State Superintendent

JUDICIAL

For Chief Judge of the Supreme Court
Shall DONALD R. WRIGHT be elected to the office for the term prescribed by law? YES / NO

For Associate Judge of the Supreme Court
Shall LOUIS H. BURKE be elected to the office for the term prescribed by law? YES / NO

For Associate Judge of the Supreme Court
Shall RAYMOND E. PETERS be elected to the office for the term prescribed by law? YES / NO

For Associate Judge of the Supreme Court
Shall RAYMOND L. SULLIVAN be elected to the office for the term prescribed by law? YES / NO

For Judge, Court of Appeal, Second Appellate District, Division One
Shall ROY A. GUSTAFSON be elected to the office for the term prescribed by law? YES / NO

For Judge, Court of Appeal, Second Appellate District, Division One
Shall MILDRED L. LILLIE be elected to the office for the term prescribed by law? YES / NO

For Judge, Court of Appeal, Second Appellate District, Division One
Shall ROBERT S. THOMPSON be elected to the office for the term prescribed by law? YES / NO

For Presiding Judge, Court of Appeal, Second Appellate District, Division Two
Shall LESTER WM. ROTH be elected to the office for the term prescribed by law? YES / NO

For Judge, Court of Appeal, Second Appellate District, Division Two
Shall LYNN D. COMPTON be elected to the office for the term prescribed by law? YES / NO

For Judge, Court of Appeal, Second Appellate District, Division Three
Shall JOHN R. ALLPORT be elected to the office for the term prescribed by law? YES / NO

For Judge, Court of Appeal, Second Appellate District, Division Three
Shall JAMES A. COBEY be elected to the office for the term prescribed by law? YES / NO

For Judge, Court of Appeal, Second Appellate District, Division Three
Shall HAROLD W. SCHWEITZER be elected to the office for the term prescribed by law? YES / NO

JUDICIAL

For Presiding Judge, Court of Appeal, Second Appellate District, Division Four
Shall GORDON L. FILES be elected to the office for the term prescribed by law? YES / NO

For Judge, Court of Appeal Second Appellate District, Division Four
Shall GEROLD C. DUNN be elected to the office for the term prescribed by law? YES / NO

For Presiding Judge, Court of Appeal, Second Appellate District, Division Five
Shall OTTO M. KAUS be elected to the office for the term prescribed by law? YES / NO

For Judge, Court of Appeal, Second Appellate District, Division Five
Shall JOHN F. AISO be elected to the office for the term prescribed by law? YES / NO

For Judge, Court of Appeal, Second Appellate District, Division Five
Shall WILLIAM A. REPPY be elected to the office for the term prescribed by law? YES / NO

For Judge, Court of Appeal, Second Appellate District, Division Five
Shall CLARKE E. STEPHENS be elected to the office for the term prescribed by law? YES / NO

COUNTY

Sheriff and Coroner — Vote for One
- JOHN W. CARPENTER — Chief of Police
- THOMAS R. THORNTON — FBI Agent, (Ret.)

MEASURES SUBMITTED TO VOTE OF VOTERS

1. THE CLEAN WATER BOND LAW OF 1970. This act provides for a bond issue of two hundred fifty million dollars ($250,000,000) to provide funds for water pollution control. FOR / AGAINST
2. VACANCIES IN SPECIFIED CONSTITUTIONAL OFFICES. Provides Supreme Court has exclusive jurisdiction to determine questions of vacancy in specified constitutional offices; authority to raise questions vested in statutory body. YES / NO
3. STATE BUDGET. Commencing in 1972, requires Governor to submit budget within first ten days of session and Legislature to adopt budget by June 15th of each year. YES / NO
4. APPROPRIATION FOR PUBLIC SCHOOLS. Authorizes Legislature to make appropriation for public schools prior to passage of budget bill if delayed. YES / NO
5. REGENTS UNIVERSITY OF CALIFORNIA: PUBLIC MEETINGS. Requires meetings of the Regents to be public, with exceptions and notice requirements as Legislature may provide. YES / NO
6. TEACHERS' RETIREMENT FUND: INVESTMENTS. Deletes exclusion of Teachers' Retirement Fund from provision authorizing investment of portion of public retirement funds in specific securities. YES / NO
7. STATE COLLEGES: SPEAKER MEMBER OF GOVERNING BODY. Provides Speaker of Assembly shall be member of State College governing body. YES / NO

MEASURES SUBMITTED TO VOTE OF VOTERS

8. SUPERINTENDENT OF PUBLIC INSTRUCTION. Authorizes one additional Deputy Superintendent of Public Instruction exempt from civil service. YES / NO
9. COUNTY SUPERINTENDENT OF SCHOOLS. Supervisors in noncharter counties may provide by ordinance approved by electorate for appointment rather than election of superintendent of schools. YES / NO
10. INTEREST RATE LIMITATION. Amends and renumbers Section 22 of Article XX of the State Constitution to provide, subject to limitations the Legislature may impose, that loans over $100,000 may be made to corporations or partnerships without regard to restrictions of such section. YES / NO
11. CHIROPRACTORS: RULES. Amendment of Chiropractic Initiative Act. Authorizes Board of Chiropractic Examiners to adopt specified rules governing chiropractics and specifies procedure. YES / NO
12. COMPENSATION OF COUNTY SUPERVISORS. Provides that county governing body shall prescribe compensation of its members by ordinance subject to referendum. YES / NO
13. TAX EXEMPTION FOR DISABLED VETERANS AND BLIND VETERANS. Increases totally disabled veteran's and widow's exemption. Extends blind veteran's exemption to home owned by corporation in which he is shareholder. YES / NO
14. STATE CIVIL SERVICE. Continues existing civil service system, revises language and removes certain provisions. Adds and removes certain positions. YES / NO
15. PARTIAL CONSTITUTIONAL REVISION. Revises, amends and repeals various miscellaneous provisions of Constitution relating to seat of government, separate property, and other matters. YES / NO
16. CONSTITUTIONAL AMENDMENTS. Authorizes Legislature to amend or withdraw proposed constitutional measures. Initiatives, referendums, and constitutional measures effective day after election. Revises procedure for constitutional convention. YES / NO
17. PARTIAL CONSTITUTIONAL REVISION. Repeals obsolete provisions relating to social welfare. YES / NO
18. MOTOR VEHICLE TAXATION AND REVENUES. Authorizes use of revenues from motor vehicle fuel tax and license fees for control of environmental pollution caused by motor vehicles; and for public transportation including mass transit systems. YES / NO
19. USURY. AMENDMENT OF USURY LAW INITIATIVE ACT. Deletes present misdemeanor penalty provisions. Adds felony penalty provisions for an unlicensed or nonexempted person charging interest in excess of limits set by law. YES / NO
20. THE RECREATION AND FISH AND WILDLIFE ENHANCEMENT BOND ACT. Provides for a bond issue of $60,000,000 to be used for planning and developing facilities for recreation and fish and wildlife enhancement. FOR / AGAINST

COUNTY

ORDINANCE REFERENDUM MEASURE

A. Shall Santa Barbara County Ordinance No. 2084, which was recommended by the County Planning Commission and approved by the Board of Supervisors and which rezones the El Capitan Ranch located west of Goleta to permit a residential and recreational development not to exceed 1,535 dwelling units on 3,638 acres, be adopted? YES / NO

CIVIL SERVICE ORDINANCE

B. Shall the resolution of the Board of Supervisors adopting a limited civil service system under the county civil service enabling law be approved? YES / NO

COUNTY OF SANTA BARBARA 112

SAMPLE BALLOT
No. 123456

FIGURE 3-2 *1970 general election ballot*

main purpose became that of endorsing candidates in the primary election. The leaders of each party learned that, under cross-filing, if a single member of the opposition party opposed two or more persons from their party in the primary, their candidates often split the vote in such a way as to enable the single candidate of the opposition party to win both nominations.

Although the CRA and CDC differ in certain respects, they have similar organizational structures, which to a remarkable degree parallel and duplicate the official party machinery. The basic units in the CRA are the local Republican assemblies, and in the CDC, the Democratic clubs. The controlling body of each organization is its state convention, which meets annually. In even-numbered years, they convene to endorse candidates for statewide elective offices, and in odd-numbered years to elect officers and directors and to discuss current issues. These state conventions—particularly those of the CDC—resemble, although on a smaller scale, the quadrennial conventions of the national parties. Party leaders address the conventions; credentials committees pass on contested seats; resolution committees draft position papers; and supporters of various candidates work for their endorsement.

The major objectives and activities of the CDC and CRA include taking stands on current issues, recruiting workers for election campaigns, and in general persuading interested individuals to participate actively in politics. The most important of their activities have been recruiting and endorsing promising candidates and providing them organizational and financial support.

Both of these unofficial organizations were remarkably successful for a number of years in securing the nominations of their endorsed candidates, but since the early 1960s the influence of each has been waning. Within the Republican party, the CRA has been confronted by more recently formed competing organizations—the United Republicans of California, the California Republican League, and the Republican Council of California. Moreover, the CRA has been plagued by internal dissension between moderates and militant conservatives. In the mid-1960s, a right-wing faction gained control of the organization. The president of the CRA acknowledged in 1966 that five of the sixteen members of the CRA executive committee were members of the John Birch Society. The CRA reportedly had a membership of approximately 13,000 in 1970.

The CDC in recent years has been embroiled in controversies with several leaders of the Democratic party. For example, in 1968 the Democratic national committeeman demanded that the CDC disband because it was "disruptive" of Democratic unity. Whereas the CRA has been charged with being more conservative than the majority of Republican voters, the CDC's stance has clearly been more liberal than that of most of the party's elected officials or rank-and-file members. CDC's membership, once reported at more than 70,000, had by 1970 fallen below 10,000. At this date, it is impossible to predict what the future of the CDC and CRA will be.

Recent history of California parties

THE REPUBLICAN ERA For more than half a century before 1958, the Republican party controlled a majority of California's elective offices. The Republicans dominated the state senate from 1891 to 1957; and, with the exception of the period from 1936 to 1942, they controlled the assembly from 1894 until 1958. For sixty years, beginning in 1898, every governor was a Republican except for Culbert L. Olson, who held the office for a single term, 1939 to 1943. From 1890 until 1958, the Democrats were able to elect only two men to the office of attorney general and were unable to elect a single person to the positions of secretary of state, treasurer, and controller. During these years, from the standpoint of state politics, California was virtually a one-party state; and often the principal struggle for political power in the state was between the two wings of the Republican party.

In presidential elections, however, California voters have closely followed the national trend. In 1916 and again from 1932 until 1952, the state's electoral vote went to the Democratic presidential nominee. On the state level, the long period of Republican hegemony in state politics was brought to a close by the overwhelming victory of the Democrats in 1958.

Republican dominance in California during the last decade of the nineteenth century and the early decades of the twentieth century were undoubtedly due in part to the popularity of the Republican party nationally. From 1896 until 1932, every President except Woodrow Wilson was a Republican, and Republican registration data showed the

TABLE 4-1 *Political party affiliation of state assembly, state senate, and House of Representatives: 1929–1971*

Session	Assembly		Senate		House of Representatives	
	REP.	DEM.	REP.	DEM.	REP.	DEM.
1929	71	9	35	5	10	1
1931	73	7	35	4	10	1
1933	54	26	35	5	9	11
1935	42	38	30	10	7	13
1937	33	47	24	16	4	16
1939	36	44	22	18	8	12
1941	38	42	24	16	9	11
1943	44	36	24	16	11	12
1945	42	37	27	13	7	16
1947	48	32	27	13	14	9
1949	45	35	26	14	13	10
1951	47	33	28	12	13	10
1953	53	27	29	11	19	11
1955	48	32	24	16	19	11
1957	42	38	20	20	17	13
1959	33	47	13	27	14	16
1961	33	47	10	30	14	16
1963	28	52	13	27	13	25
1965	31	49	13	27	15	23
1967	38	42	19	21	17	21
1969	41	39	21	19	17	21
1971	37	43	19	21	18	20

Republicans greatly outnumbering the Democrats. Since 1934, however, the Democratic registration has exceeded that of the Republicans by a sizable margin (see Figure 4-2). In 1970, there were 4,781,282 registered Democrats and 3,469,046 registered Republicans.[3]

One question that has intrigued many Californians is how the Republicans were able to dominate the state political scene after the Democrats became the majority party. The answer lies in a combination of factors and circumstances. (1) At least until after the creation

[3] At the time of the 1970 general election, 66,936 persons were registered as members of the American Independent Party, and 41,663 were registered in the Peace and Freedom Party.

of the California Democratic Council, the Republicans were more effective than the Democrats in selecting candidates and in organizing support for them. Due largely to the efforts of the California Republican Assembly, Republican candidates were generally better known and also were given more financial and organizational support than were Democratic candidates. (2) In most cases, the Republicans had the advantage of being incumbents. This meant that they were listed first on the ballot with the word "incumbent" appearing after their names. (3) Being in control of the state legislature, the Republicans also had the opportunity to gerrymander the state to their advantage following every decennial census. (4) The majority of the newspapers in the state have favored the Republican party, both on their editorial pages and in their news columns. For example, it has been estimated that of California's newspapers, 80 percent have been Republican in orientation, 10 percent Democratic, and 10 percent independent.[4] In any state, but especially where a sizable number of voters are recent arrivals and where campaigns are largely waged in the mass media, newspaper support is obviously of great value to a party. In addition, in California party registration is a misleading index of the electoral strength of a party. Typically, of the registered voters, 5 to 10 percent fewer Democrats vote in an election than Republicans; and members of both parties cross party lines and vote for candidates of the opposite party.

THE DEMOCRATS IN POWER   In 1958, the Democrats won a spectacular victory, electing majorities in both houses of the legislature, a majority of California congressmen, a United States senator, the governor, and every other statewide elective officer except the secretary of state. This landslide was due to several factors and events. A nationwide Democratic trend that year undoubtedly had some impact on California. The decision of Senator William Knowland to run for governor and of Governor Goodwin Knight to run for the United States Senate deprived the Republicans of the advantage of having incumbents running for reelection for the two top offices. Senator Knowland's espousal of the antiunion "right-to-work" initiative measure undoubtedly contributed to his defeat and had an adverse effect on the entire Republican ticket.

[4] James E. Gregg, "Newspaper Editorial Endorsements and California Elections," *Journalism Quarterly*, vol. 42, no. 4, pp. 532–538, Autumn, 1965.

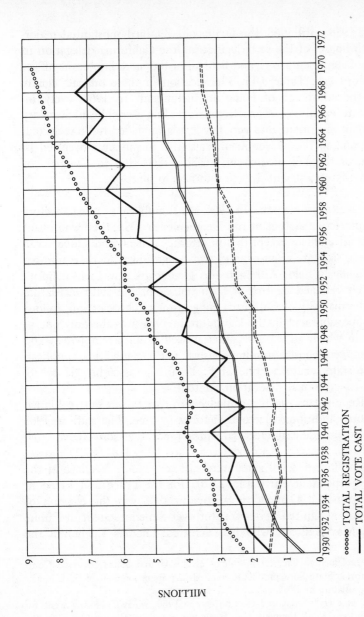

ooooo TOTAL REGISTRATION
—— TOTAL VOTE CAST
══ DEMOCRATIC REGISTRATION
==== REPUBLICAN REGISRATION

FIGURE 4-2 *Voting and party registration, 1930–1970*

MILLIONS

79

From 1958 until 1966, the Democrats retained substantial majorities in both houses of the state legislature, the California delegation in the House of Representatives, and held all of the more important offices in Sacramento (see Table 4-1). The election of these officials clearly illustrates the advantage of being an incumbent. In 1962, every incumbent state executive was reelected including Republican Secretary of State Frank M. Jordan, and very few legislators failed to be reelected. The high point in the reelection of legislative incumbents occurred in 1964 when, of the 132 incumbents seeking reelection to Congress or the state legislature, all but 2 were returned to office.

THE REPUBLICAN RESURGENCE   In 1966, the Republicans scored a victory almost as impressive as that of the Democrats in 1958; they won all of the top executive offices except that of attorney general and added seven assemblymen, six state senators, and two congressmen to their number of seats previously held. Although the Democrats saw their majority reduced, they retained control of both houses of the state legislature and elected a majority of California congressmen. This election, following the reapportionment of the legislature in 1965, was the only one in forty years in which all state senators as well as all assemblymen and congressmen were chosen simultaneously.[5] The Democratic-Republican ratio in the state senate became 21 to 19; in the assembly, 42 to 38; and in the congressional delegation, 21 to 17.

The Republicans, having gained control of the executive branch in 1966, scored additional electoral victories in 1968. The state in 1968 cast its forty presidential electoral votes for native son Richard M. Nixon.[6] Nixon received 3,467,664 votes to 3,244,318 for Democrat Hubert Humphrey; 438,270 votes were cast for George Wallace of the American Independent Party and 27,707 for the Peace and Freedom Party. The principal Democratic victory in 1968 was the election of Alan Cranston as United States senator over Superintendent of Public Instruction Max Rafferty, who had defeated Thomas Kuchel in the

[5] As will be explained in Chapter 5, rulings of the United States Supreme Court and the California State Supreme Court resulted in reapportionment of both houses of the state legislature in 1965.
[6] Since 1912, in every presidential election except 1960, when California went for Nixon rather than John Kennedy, the state has given its electoral vote to the winning presidential candidate.

Republican primary. As for strength in the legislature, the Republicans gained three assembly seats in 1968 to give their party a 41 to 39 majority in that house. The advantage of being an incumbent was again illustrated as all twenty state senators whose terms expired were re-elected, as were the thirty-seven congressmen seeking reelection. In 1969, a by-election to fill a state senate vacancy caused by the death of a Democratic senator was won by a Republican, giving the Republicans control of both houses for the first time in fourteen years.

What accounts for these Republican electoral victories? In 1966, some voters apparently felt that two terms were sufficient for Governor Brown, while others supported the out-party (the Republicans) as a means of indicating their discontent over such problems as the war in Vietnam and street and campus demonstrations. In addition, Reagan's professionally conducted campaign was better organized and more effective than his opponent's, and his landslide victory helped sweep other Republicans into office.

Governor Reagan has been a great asset to the Republicans of California. Although professing not to be a "politician," he has been one of the most effective and sophisticated campaigners the state has ever seen. Under him the Republicans have achieved a united front, whereas from 1962 the Democrats were handicapped by factionalism and the unwillingness of certain party leaders—including Los Angeles Mayor Samuel Yorty and former Speaker Jesse M. Unruh—to support Democratic candidates. The Republicans have experienced less difficulty than the Democrats in raising campaign funds. Although some Democratic candidates have had enough money to wage strong campaigns, generally speaking, the Democratic campaign committees have had insufficient financial resources. With their more ample funds, the Republicans have been able to make far greater use of professional campaign management firms, to have larger and better staffs, and to conduct more effective campaigns.

Under the Republican CAL-Plan (Capture the Legislature Plan), the GOP state central committee in every recent election has zeroed in on certain assembly and senate seats held by Democrats and has made an all-out effort to win them. These expertly conducted campaigns have involved the taking of public opinion polls, the hiring of campaign management firms, and the recruitment of unusually large numbers of campaign workers. Evidence of the success of CAL-Plan lies in the fact that by employing it the Republicans gained enough seats by 1969 to obtain majorities in both houses of the legislature.

The 1970 election produced mixed results. The Republicans re-elected Governor Reagan and all incumbent statewide executive officers. The two executive positions to which incumbents were not seeking reelection were divided between the parties with a Republican winning the office of attorney general and a Democrat (for the first time this century) being elected secretary of state. Former movie actor George Murphy was defeated in his bid for a second term in the United States Senate by Democrat John V. Tunney. Thus for the first time since the Civil War both of California's United States Senators were Democrats. In the contest for the nonpartisan office of superintendent of public instruction, Wilson Riles defeated incumbent Max Rafferty. Although the Republicans elected one additional congressman, the Democrats maintained a 20 to 18 margin in the House of Representatives. To the surprise of most political observers the Democrats recaptured control of both houses of the state legislature, making a net gain of four assemblymen and two state senators. These gains gave them a majority of 43 to 37 in the assembly and 21 to 19 in the senate.

POLITICAL-INTEREST GROUPS

Various terms or phrases are employed to describe the private organizations or groups that attempt to influence government. Those most commonly used are "political-interest groups" or "pressure groups," but some people prefer to call them "interest groups," "special interests," or "lobbies." Groups of this type have been active in California since its early history. They are a normal part of civic life in a free society and should be recognized as intrinsic elements in our political system. Probably in no other state is there such a variety of active and influential political-interest groups as there is in California.

Political-interest groups classified

Largely because of the diversity of the political-interest or pressure groups, no completely satisfactory classification of such groups has been devised. However, for the purpose of this analysis, they can be placed into three categories.

First, there is the semiofficial lobby composed of governmental agencies and organizations of public officials and employees. Included in this category are state administrative agencies and departments, individual cities and counties that send legislative advocates to the capital, and organizations such as the California State Employees' Association, California Teachers Association, League of California Cities, and California State Sheriffs Association. The lobbying activities of these groups in the first category are usually related to securing legislation or the appropriation of funds for some state or local government program or activity.

The second category is composed of miscellaneous nongovernmental organizations whose legislative aims vary widely but all of which are apparently interested in legislation for other than economic reasons. Examples of such organizations are the American Civil Liberties Union, the Friends Committee on Legislation, the Sierra Club, and the League of Women Voters of California.

The third category of lobby organizations encompasses the heterogeneous nongovernmental associations, corporations, firms, and groups that have an economic stake in the action of the legislature. Most numerous are the representatives of business. Virtually every trade association and many individual firms and corporations have one or more lobbyists in the capital during legislative sessions. Examples of the types of business organizations represented are the California State Chamber of Commerce, California Brewers Association, California Retailers Association, Malt Beverage Industry, Association of Independent Oil Producers, California Motor Transport Association, Pacific Gas and Electric Company, and Association of Motion Picture and Television Producers, and the Union Oil Company.

Organizations that represent agriculture, labor, and the professions and that employ lobbyists also are classed in the third category. Examples of these organizations are the California Farm Bureau Federation, California State Federation of Labor, California Teamsters Legislative Council, the bar, and medical and dental associations.

Functions and criticisms of political-interest groups

Political-interest groups in general perform certain useful functions: (1) They provide a type of group representation. When the activities and interests of the people become highly diversified, as they are in most parts of California, it becomes very difficult for an elected representative to know the views of all different groups of people who live in his constituency. Groups are thus organized to speak for and represent their members. (2) Interest groups help to inform the people on political issues and to stimulate discussion of those issues. (3) They provide public officials with much useful information.

There are, however, certain criticisms of interest-group activities: (1) All individuals are not members of organized groups, and those who are not organized are placed at a disadvantage. (2) Some groups are better organized and have greater financial resources than others and tend to exert influence out of proportion to the number of their members. (3) It is not always clear who is represented by an organized group. An organization may have an impressive name and purport to represent hundreds of individuals, but it may be merely a "front" organization supported by individuals who do not want their identity to be known. (4) Some pressure groups use methods and techniques inimical to the proper functioning of democratic government.

Pressure politics in the past

The pattern of pressure-group politics has varied considerably during California's history. By 1870, the influence of the Central Pacific Railroad and its builders—Charles Crocker, Mark Hopkins, Collis P. Huntington, and Leland Stanford—was beginning to be felt in the state. This railroad, reorganized as the Southern Pacific, was the dominant force in California politics for nearly four decades. A leading historian of the period has written: "To a degree perhaps unparalleled in the nation, the Southern Pacific and a web of associated economic interests ruled the state."[7] Principal credit for ending the political domination of the Southern Pacific must go to the Progressive reformers elected to office in 1910. The political reforms enacted by the Progressives not only broke the stranglehold of the Southern Pacific but, as has been explained, also weakened the political parties.

Into the political vacuum thus created moved a variety of organized business, agricultural, labor, professional, and social-reform

[7] George E. Mowry, *The California Progressives*, Berkeley: University of California Press, 1951, p. 9.

groups. Of the various lobbyists employed by these groups, one, Arthur H. Samish, became highly influential in state politics. His political power stemmed in large part from the vast amount of money placed at his disposal by organized interests employing him, which included beer and liquor companies and, at times, banks, race tracks, railroads, bus and truck lines, and tobacco firms. Samish's influence in politics was brought to an end in 1953 when he was sentenced to prison for violation of the federal income tax law. No individual has since acquired anything like the power and influence he exercised; but, as one writer on California politics has observed, it must not be supposed that the lobbyists no longer "wield important influence in the California Legislature."

Interest-group strategy

The manner in which interest groups operate is determined largely by the political environment. In California, the legal restrictions under which political parties are forced to operate have weakened their official organizations and thus indirectly enlarged the role interest groups are able to play in practical politics. In addition, the great diversity in economic life; the highly developed business, labor, farm, and professional associations; and the great variety of other organized groups have also enhanced the importance of pressure-group activity. Depending on the objectives and characteristics of the particular organization—its size, financial resources, and cohesiveness—an interest group may attempt in a variety of ways to influence decisions made by the government.

INFLUENCING NOMINATIONS AND ELECTIONS Much of the influence of political-interest groups results from their participation in the nomination and election of public officials. As noted above, pressure groups are nonpartisan groups; they do not themselves draft party platforms or directly nominate candidates for public office. Many organized groups do, however, attempt to get one or both of the major parties to endorse particular policies, and many play an active role in nomination and election campaigns. Indeed, in nonpartisan elections, political-interest groups do virtually everything that parties do in partisan elections except nominate candidates on a ticket of their own.

In general, the groups that are most active in the electoral process are those able to wield substantial influence through the media of mass communications, through a large membership of voters, or by providing campaign contributions or workers. One such group is organized labor. For example, the head of the AFL-CIO Committee on Political Education in Los Angeles announced before the 1966 campaign the establishment of a steering committee, which would have as its purpose: "jointly screening candidates, ironing out differences to avoid conflict, allocating finances, and funneling in campaign workers on the basis of need for each individual candidate."

The most common method used by organized interests to aid a campaign is that of financial contributions.[8] In the words of a California oil lobbyist: "These people [public officials] don't get elected by accident, simply on their own steam. . . . We give them checks. The contributions," he added, "are made on the basis of a man's record." One group of conservative businessmen known as "United for California" reportedly contributes as much as $300,000 every election year to a campaign fund for conservative candidates for the state legislature. According to one account, a dozen lobbyists for conservative groups analyze legislative races and recommend which candidates should receive financial support.[9]

In addition to direct financial contributions, it is not uncommon for organized groups to aid in campaigns by permitting candidates and party officials to use offices and equipment without charge; by supporting candidates by television, radio, billboard, and newspaper advertisements; and by paying salaries to officers and employees working full or part time for a party or candidate. There have been instances when a pressure group has had its lobbyist or political counsel help direct election campaigns.

INFLUENCING PUBLIC OPINION   Organized interest groups use the media of mass communication to conduct public relations campaigns aimed at informing and propagandizing the public. One of the methods used to shape public attitudes is institutional advertising, which may be de-

[8] For example, the reports of campaign contributions filed in 1968 by a leading state senator, included the names of eighteen well-known registered lobbyists.
[9] Robert Fairbanks, "State Lobbying: Skullduggery Is Slowly Fading," *Los Angeles Times*, Apr. 23, 1969, pt. I, p. 22.

fined as the use of paid space or time in the communication media to promote or oppose ideas rather than to sell products. To inform or to "educate" the electorate regarding some public policy or proposal, professional public relations or advertising personnel are often employed; and television and radio programs, newspaper advertising and editorials, leaflets, pamphlets, and even books are utilized. They expect the voters as a result to influence public officials.

In recent years *demonstration politics* has been employed more than in any previous era to exert influence on both public opinion and public officials. Through rallies, parades, extended marches, strikes, and boycotts people have called attention to what they consider to be important political issues or grievances. Such methods were first used primarily by civil-rights groups and the peace movement. In the late 1960s in California, demonstration politics was used increasingly as a tactical method of such groups as teachers, college students, doctors, police officers, and other public employees. For instance, college students have marched on Sacramento and have demonstrated in various cities and on college campuses to protest such matters as budgetary cuts for the state colleges and university, the dismissal of college teachers, and the protracted war in Southeast Asia. Various groups have sought by mass exhibitions to express the fervor and depth of their convictions.

PRESSURES ON THE LEGISLATURE The term "lobby" has been used to designate pressure groups seeking the enactment or defeat of legislation. In recent years in California registered lobbyists—officially referred to as "legislative advocates"—have outnumbered the legislators by more than 4 to 1. There are two different and distinct types of lobbyists: (1) the full-time employee or officer of an organization, trade association, or other group, who stays in Sacramento during legislative sessions and is engaged in other activities for his organization the remainder of the year; and (2) the lobbyist-for-hire, who may be employed by several firms or associations at one time and who may change clients from session to session. In general, the former are usually more highly respected and are better informed regarding the organizations they represent, whereas the latter rely to a greater extent on personal influence. (See Figure 4-3.)

The popular references to the lobby as the "third house" give some indication of the influence of these interest groups on the legislative

1162

FORM 3

MONTHLY REPORT OF PERSONS REGISTERED UNDER STATUTE REGULATING LEGISLATIVE REPRESENTATION TO BE FILED WITH THE LEGISLATIVE ANALYST WHO IS DESIGNATED SO TO ACT, BY SENATE RULE 9.7 AND ASSEMBLY RULE 30. THIS REPORT SHOULD BE FILED BETWEEN THE FIRST AND FIFTEENTH DAY OF EACH CALENDAR MONTH FOR EACH MONTH SO LONG AS THE REGISTRANT'S ACTIVITY CONTINUES.

Date April 10/68 For month ending March 31, 1968 Month of last report February, 1968

Registrant's name JAMES D. GARIBALDI

Business Address 510 West 6th St., Los Angeles, Calif. 90014

Sacramento Address Senator Hotel

In whose interest you are reporting: See attached list

Filed With
Legislative Budget Committee

APR 11 1968

(1) Report of all money received during preceding calendar month:

Salaries, fees, retainers: $ 5,998.47

Reimbursement of expenses: $ 6,067.98

(2) Detailed report of each expenditure of $25 or more. Describe in detail. Supplementary report sheets are available.

To Whom Paid	Purpose	Amount
See attached list		$
		$
		$
		$
		$

Payments in your behalf made directly by your employer $ None

(3) Total of all expenditures during the preceding calendar month $ 6,067.98

(4) The names of all papers, periodicals, magazines, radio or television, or other publications in which you have caused to be published or made public any articles, advertisements or editorials.

None

(5) The pending or proposed legislation you are employed to support or oppose:

All legislation affecting the race tracks, wholesale beverage distributors, highway petrolmen, outdoor advertising, trading stamps, oil companies, and court reporters.

...I declare under penalty of perjury that the foregoing is true and correct.
(See Section 2015.5, C.C.P.)

(Signature of Registrant)

1163

JAMES D. GARIBALDI - Form 3

Names and addresses of employers:

Hollywood Turf Club	South Prairie Ave., Inglewood, Calif.
California Wholesale Beverage Distributors Association	55 New Montgomery St., San Francisco
Blue Chip Stamp Company	5801 S. Western Ave., Los Angeles
Pacific Outdoor Advertising Co.	P O Box 3199, Term.Ap.Los Angeles, Calif.
Signal Oil and Gas Co.	P O Box 17126 Los Angeles, Calif. 9001 T
California Assn. of Highway Petrolmen	P O Box 831, Pleasant Hill, California
California Court Reporters Association	c/o Susan Embini, Secretary-Treasurer P O Box 156, Richmond, Calif. 9408

Detailed report of each expenditure of $25 or more:

To whom paid	Purpose	Amount
Senator Hotel	Rent, meals, beverages, telephone etc.	$ 2,476.30
Corum's	Beverages	1,010.41
Pacific Telephone	Local and long distance calls	172.70
Sallee Svilich	Clerical assistance	50.00
	Postage	28.00
Tan Tan Cafe	Meals and beverages	284.62
Connoisseur Wine Imports	Beverages	192.11
Dick Posey's Cottage	Meals and beverages	90.05
Aldo's, Inc.	"	130.25
Antonina's	"	77.00
Sacramento Inn	"	171.97
Frank Fat's	"	57.82
The Rum	"	86.28
Blum's	"	403.45
The Fire House	"	34.96
Machiavelli's	"	330.04
El Mirador Hotel	"	
		$ 6,067.98

FIGURE 4-3 *This monthly report by a leading lobbyist shows his salary, expenditures, and employees*

process. In comparison with the legislators themselves, the experienced lobbyists tend to receive higher salaries,[10] to have a wider knowledge of the legislative process, and to be better informed on the issues of greatest concern to their clients. A number of legislators have become lobbyists after serving in the assembly or senate. In one year, for example, the registered lobbyists included fourteen former state legislators, a former congressman, and six former directors of state departments. Former speakers of the assembly have returned to the capital as registered lobbyists, and at least two assemblymen have resigned from the legislature to accept higher-paying positions as lobbyists.

Generally speaking, the most active and influential lobby groups are those having a direct economic interest in legislation. These groups vary widely, however, in the extent of their activities. Some are interested in only a few bills. Others take stands on a wide variety of legislative measures and are active in politics on a year-round basis. In 1969, the top staff members assigned to legislative committees listed the "liquor lobby" and "horseracing interests" as being the most active lobby groups. In an earlier survey, California legislators ranked the most influential lobby groups: California Teachers Association, AFL-CIO, California Farm Bureau, California Medical Association, League

[10] The top lobbyists receive from $25,000 to $75,000 a year plus a generous expense account for entertainment.

"The Small Society" (Reprinted by permission of Brickman and the Washington Star Syndicate)

of California Cities, and the Chamber of Commerce.[11] Such an association normally has one or more full-time employees whose principal function is to look after its political interests in Sacramento. These individuals are usually in the capital lobbying on bills throughout the legislative sessions. When the legislature is not in session, they commonly serve as public relations counselors, attorneys, or executive directors for their organizations.

Naturally, the most important work of the lobbyist is done during legislative sessions. Bills sponsored by his organization are given to legislators to be introduced. These measures are then watched carefully as they proceed through the various stages of the legislative process to see that they are acted upon by both houses. A lobbyist also wants to ensure that no legislation hostile to the interests of his group is enacted. Many organizations have staff members read every bill introduced to determine which should be supported and which opposed. Most lobbyists concentrate their attention at the committee level both because it is easier to influence a smaller group than the entire membership and because assemblymen and senators commonly accept committee recommendations regarding bills.

Pressure groups and their lobbyists attempt in various ways to win support for the bills their organizations favor and to defeat those they oppose. Most legislative advocates insist that the most effective method is to present honestly and candidly information supporting their position. Legislative advocates commonly testify during committee hearings and discuss measures privately with individual legislators.

In the past, some organizations have obtained the votes of legislators through bribes, gifts, entertainment, retainer fees, and promises of subsequent employment. Although accounts and rumors of such practices have been heard less frequently in recent years, it would be incorrect to assume that none of these methods are still being used.[12] Cali-

---

[11] John C. Wahlke, Heinz Eulau, William Buchanan, and LeRoy C. Ferguson, *The Legislative System*, New York: John Wiley & Sons, Inc., 1962, pp. 318–319.

[12] In 1970, the press reported that a state senator had accepted a check for $5,000 from the California Association of Thrift and Loan Companies one day after a bill in which the association was interested was assigned to a committee of which he was then vice-chairman. The senator stated that the check was a campaign contribution, although his term in office did not expire for 3½ years. An official of the association said the money was given in hopes of "expediting" committee approval of the bill. *Los Angeles Times*, Mar. 11, 1970.

fornia lawmakers probably have more opportunities than any other group of legislators to have lobbyists pay for their meals, drinks, and entertainment. Almost any day during legislative sessions, lawmakers may choose among luncheons paid for by lobbyists. Groups also occasionally make veiled promises of support or reprisal in future elections. Some lobbyists stimulate communications from the constituents of legislators they hope to influence. One method commonly used is that of inducing several influential persons from a legislator's district to call or write him; another is to persuade a large number of constituents to flood him with postcards, telegrams, and letters urging a certain course of action.

As legislation favoring one organized interest may appear harmful to another, lobby groups often find themselves pitted against one another. For instance, bills to increase unemployment compensation may bring organized labor into conflict with business organizations. On the other hand, lobbyists often find it possible to make common cause with each other. For instance, on one occasion, the press reported that some two dozen lobbyists had met together to consider joint action aimed at defeating certain of Governor Brown's taxation proposals. Some groups actually work together on a semipermanent basis, for example, the so-called highway lobby, composed of lobbyists representing contractors, oil companies, automakers, and truckers.

PRESSURES ON EXECUTIVES AND JUDICIAL OFFICIALS Political-interest groups and their lobbyists do not, of course, limit their efforts to attempting to influence the legislative branch of the government. After bills have been passed by both houses of the legislature, interest groups attempt to get the governor to sign or to veto them. If lobby groups fail to secure the desired action from the legislature and governor, they occasionally make use of the initiative or referendum. Organized interest groups also exert pressure directly or indirectly on administrative agencies. They strive to have "friendly" officials appointed to agencies that administer laws affecting them and to secure decisions and actions by those agencies that favor their organizations.

Although pressure organizations expend considerably less energy and time attempting to influence the judicial branch of the government than either the executive or legislative branch, efforts are made to influence the courts. Occasionally groups seek to advance the cause of their members by initiating litigation to test the constitutionality of actions of public officials, statutes passed by the legislature, or measures adopted through the initiative. For instance, after Proposition 14, an initiative constitutional amendment, was placed on the ballot by members of the California Real Estate Association and approved by the voters in 1964, individuals and groups opposing the measure succeeded in having it tested before the state supreme court, which in 1966 declared the proposition in conflict with provisions of the federal Constitution and therefore invalid.

Interest-group regulation

The California Lobbying Act, based on the Federal Regulation of Lobbying Act of 1946, has as its primary aim providing the legislators and the citizenry of the state information concerning lobbyist activities. The act applies to two classes of persons: (1) the paid lobbyists labeled by the act as "legislative advocates" and (2) other individuals and groups whose purpose is the influencing of legislation.

Each lobbyist, or legislative advocate, must register with the legislative analyst and file monthly reports listing the bills he has been employed to support or oppose, all money he has received, and each expenditure of $25 or more. Excluded from this requirement are public officials acting in an official capacity, persons merely testifying before committees, representatives of churches, and newspaper personnel.

The second group covered by the act includes any "individual, partnership, committee, corporation, and any other organization or group of persons" soliciting or receiving "money or any other thing of value" to be used to aid in the enactment or defeat of any legislation. These individuals and groups must file statements listing every contribution of $100 or more, all expenditures of $25 or more, and the total amount spent. Lists of the legislative advocates, the organizations they represent, and the reports filed by them are published periodically in the assembly and senate *Journals*.

Some years ago an assembly committee, which had investigated the operation of the lobby laws, recommended that the statutes should be amended with the objective of forcing increased disclosure of the sources, amounts, and uses of money spent to influence legislation; of requiring clearer identification of individuals, firms, institutions, and associations attempting to influence legislation; and of maintaining a high standard of ethics among professional legislative advocates. All of these proposals are desirable, but they do not go far enough. In addition, some independent official or agency should be responsible for analyzing the lobbyists' reports and publicizing the information in a form that would enable both the public and the legislators to understand more fully the activities and aims of lobby groups. Finally, individuals appearing before administrative agencies should also be required to register before their appearances and subsequently to file statements revealing their expenditures.

CHAPTER 5

ℭHE LEGISLATURE

The California state legislature has as its primary function the determination of public policy through the enactment of law. By enacting statutory measures, the legislature decides what the government will do, creates the agencies that will perform the various activities, and determines the amount of money to be spent by each agency as well as how the money is to be raised. Not all lawmaking functions, however, are vested in the state legislature. The governor, as a policy formulator, is the chief legislator; many administrative agencies have authority to make rules and regulations having the force of law; and the courts through their decisions also play a vital role in establishing public policy. Moreover, the voters may directly enact legislation through the initiative and nullify it by the referendum.

STRUCTURE OF THE LEGISLATURE

California has a bicameral, or two-house, legislature, as do all other states except Nebraska. The assembly has eighty members elected for two-year terms. The upper house, or senate, consists of forty members elected for four-year terms, half of them being elected every two years.

Apportionment

Since California entered the Union, assembly districts have been based on population; and, until 1926, the forty senatorial districts were also established on a population basis, with each senatorial district comprising two assembly districts. Opposition to this arrangement began to develop about 1910 when it became evident that the urban population of southern California was growing faster than the population of other parts of the state and that control of the legislature might soon pass from the residents of the San Francisco area and the rural northern counties to the southern part of the state.

The California constitution enjoins the legislature to reapportion the state following each federal decennial census. After the 1920 census, the legislature was unable in three general sessions to agree on a reapportionment of the legislature. The impasse was broken in 1926 when certain groups in the rural parts of the state and the San Francisco Bay region joined forces to secure the adoption, by constitutional amendment, of the so-called federal plan of apportionment. This scheme provided for representation in the senate to be based on forty geographic districts so constituted that no county would have more than one senatorial district and no more than three counties would be grouped together to form a senatorial district. Under this system, southern California and all heavily populated counties were greatly underrepresented in the state senate. For example, in 1965, the four most populous counties of southern California—Los Angeles, San Diego, Orange, and San Bernardino—had more than 50 percent of the people in the state, but only 10 percent of the seats in the senate.

Efforts were made in 1948, 1960, and 1962 through constitutional initiatives to reapportion the senate on a modified population basis, but all of them failed. Finally, reapportionment of the state senate was achieved as a result of judicial decisions. In 1962, the United States

Supreme Court ruled, in the case of *Baker v. Carr* (369 U.S. 186), that the equal protection clause of the Fourteenth Amendment to the federal Constitution could be invoked to test the fairness of representation in a state legislature. Two years later, in *Reynolds v. Sims* (377 U.S. 533), the Court carried its earlier decision to its logical conclusion and ruled that both houses of a state legislature "must be apportioned according to population." As a result of that decision, the California Supreme Court in 1965 directed the legislature to reapportion the state senate on the principle of "one man, one vote"; and this has been the rule for both houses since that time.

The politics of legislative apportionment

After each decennial federal census, the state legislature has the responsibility for reapportioning congressional districts as well as the state senate and assembly districts.[1] Whereas the number of senate and assembly districts has remained constant, California's representation in Congress has increased every ten years. Following the 1970 census, California received five additional seats in the House of Representatives, giving the state a total of forty-three, the largest of any state.

Dividing California into the various senate, assembly, and congressional districts is a complicated task and one in which politics plays an important role. In drawing the several sets of boundaries, consideration is naturally given to political, socioeconomic, and geographical factors as well as the desires of the residents. The wishes of incumbent assemblymen and state senators are sought, partly because any apportionment measure must be approved by a majority vote in each house of the state legislature.[2] Although legislative districts must be drawn according to the "one man, one vote" principle, exact mathematical precision is not required; and political parties have found that the districts can still be gerrymandered for the advantage of the party in power. This has been done by spreading the known support of the party

[1] The constitutional amendment adopted in 1926 provides that if the legislature fails to reapportion the districts following a federal decennial census, they would be apportioned by a commission consisting of the lieutenant governor, attorney general, controller, secretary of state, and superintendent of public instruction.
[2] In drawing congressional district boundaries, the wishes of incumbent congressmen are usually sought.

in power to provide winning margins in as many districts as possible and concentrating the voting strength of the opposition in a comparatively few districts. This process often produces "safe" districts for the opposition party as well as the party in control of the legislature. During the 1960s, more than half of the legislative districts in California were considered "safe" for one or the other of the two parties. In order to give the maximum advantage to the party in power, district boundaries are commonly drawn to include certain socioeconomic groups and to exclude others; this, plus the desire to please incumbent legislators, accounts in large part for the ludicrous appearance of most maps showing assembly, state senatorial, or congressional districts (see Figures 5-1, 5-2, and 5-3). Both parties made strong efforts to elect assemblymen and state senators in 1970, knowing that the party controlling the legislature in 1971 would design the constituencies for the next decade.

Reapportioning the legislative districts would be simplified if congressional districts were also utilized for state legislative districts. This could be done by amending the state constitution to provide that after each decennial census the state legislators would increase so that there would be the same number of state senators and congressmen and the number of assemblymen would be twice the number of congressmen. Congressional and state senate districts could then be identical and each could be divided to form two assembly districts. In addition to simplifying reapportionment, one advantage of this proposal would be that as California's population continues to grow, relative to that of the rest of the country, the number of assemblymen and state senators would increase and they would seem more accessible to individual citizens. One continuing problem under any apportionment plan, however, is that although districts may be equal in population at the time of reapportionment, they may soon vary considerably because of the unequal rates of growth in different parts of the state.

Legislative sessions

Two kinds of legislative sessions may be held in California: general sessions and special sessions.[3] General sessions commence on the first

[3] Under the 1879 constitution, general sessions of 120 days were originally held biennially in odd-numbered years. In 1946 the constitution was amended to provide a budget session of thirty days in even-numbered years. General and budget sessions

Monday after the first day of January. Bills may be introduced any time during the session, subject to the provision that no bill except the budget bill may be acted upon until thirty days after introduction unless approval is granted by a vote of three-quarters of the house. The legislature during the two-year term of assemblymen is not considered a continuous body, as Congress is a continuous body during the two-year terms of members of the House of Representatives. Bills not passed during the first general session of the California Legislature are dead and are not carried over to the second general session, as they are in Congress; to be enacted they must be reintroduced.

The governor may call special sessions at any time, and during special sessions the legislature may consider only the subject or subjects specified by the governor in his call. Numerous special sessions were held prior to 1966 when general sessions occurred only in odd-numbered years. Since the establishment of annual general sessions there has been less need for special sessions and few have been called.

Qualifications and compensations of legislators

Members of the legislature must be citizens more than twenty-one years of age and must have been residents of the state for at least three years and of their respective districts for at least one year. Before 1966, the salaries of legislators were written into the constitution and could be changed only by amendment. Legislators were paid $1,200 before 1949; $3,600 from then until 1954; and $6,000 from that date until 1967. Constitutional revision in 1966 authorized members of the legislature to fix their own salaries by a two-thirds vote, and to increase them subsequently by as much as 5 percent a year. Taking immediate advantage of the new rule, they first raised their salaries to $16,000 annually in 1967 and in 1969 voted to increase them to $19,200.

In addition to his salary, every legislator receives a per diem tax-free expense allowance while the legislature is in session or while

---

in alternate years were continued until the adoption of the 1966 constitutional revision, which eliminated the budget sessions and established annual general sessions of unlimited duration. In 1970 the legislature was in session for 229 calendar days, the longest in California history. Of that time the senate actually met 147 days and the assembly 138.

1. Del Norte, Humboldt, Marin, Mendocino, Napa, Sonoma
2. Alpine, Amador, Butte, Calaveras, El Dorado, Inyo, Lassen, Madera, Mariposa, Modoc, Mono, Nevada, Placer, Plumas, Shasta, Sierra, Siskiyou, Tehama, Trinity, Tuolumne
3. Sacramento
4. Colusa, Glenn, Lake, Sacramento, Solano, Sutter, Yolo, Yuba
5. San Francisco
6. Marin, San Francisco
7-8 Alameda

9. Alameda, San Mateo, Santa Clara
10: San Benito, Santa Clara
11. San Mateo
12. Kings, Monterey, San Luis Obispo, Santa Cruz
13. Los Angeles, Santa Barbara, Ventura
14. Contra Costa
15. Merced, San Joaquin, Stanislaus
16. Fresno, Merced
17. Los Angeles
18. Kern, Tulare
19-23. Los Angeles
24. Los Angeles, San Bernardino
25. Los Angeles, Orange
26. Los Angeles
27. Kern, Los Angeles
28-31. Los Angeles
32. Los Angeles, Orange
33. San Bernardino
34. Los Angeles, Orange
35. Orange, San Diego
36-37. San Diego
38. Imperial, Riverside, San Bernardino

FIGURE 5-1   *Congressional districts, 1968–1971*

1. Del Norte, Humboldt, Lake, Mendocino, Siskiyou, Sonoma, Trinity
2. Butte, Colusa, Glenn, Shasta, Sutter, Tehama, Yolo, Yuba, Solano
3. Alpine, Amador, Calaveras, El Dorado, Lassen, Modoc, Nevada, Placer, Plumas, Sierra
4. Marin, Napa, Solano
5. Sacramento
6. Sacramento, San Joaquin
7. Contra Costa
8. Alameda
9-10. San Francisco
11. Alameda
12. San Mateo
13. Santa Clara
14. Santa Clara, Alameda
15. Inyo, Madera, Mariposa, Merced, Mono, Tulare, Fresno
16. Fresno
17. Monterey, San Benito, San Luis Obispo, Santa Cruz
18. Kern, Kings
19. Los Angeles
20. San Bernardino
21-23. Los Angeles
24. Santa Barbara, Ventura
25-33. Los Angeles
34. Orange
35. Orange, Los Angeles
36. Riverside, San Bernardino
37. Los Angeles
38-39. San Diego
40. San Diego, Imperial

FIGURE 5-2 *Senatorial districts, 1966–1971*

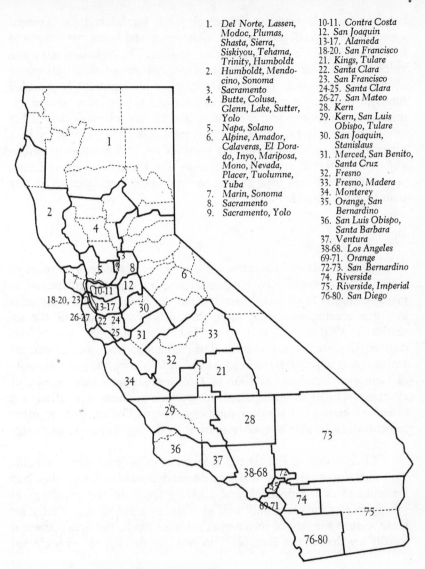

1. Del Norte, Lassen, Modoc, Plumas, Shasta, Sierra, Siskiyou, Tehama, Trinity, Humboldt
2. Humboldt, Mendocino, Sonoma
3. Sacramento
4. Butte, Colusa, Glenn, Lake, Sutter, Yolo
5. Napa, Solano
6. Alpine, Amador, Calaveras, El Dorado, Inyo, Mariposa, Mono, Nevada, Placer, Tuolumne, Yuba
7. Marin, Sonoma
8. Sacramento
9. Sacramento, Yolo

10-11. Contra Costa
12. San Joaquin
13-17. Alameda
18-20. San Francisco
21. Kings, Tulare
22. Santa Clara
23. San Francisco
24-25. Santa Clara
26-27. San Mateo
28. Kern
29. Kern, San Luis Obispo, Tulare
30. San Joaquin, Stanislaus
31. Merced, San Benito, Santa Cruz
32. Fresno
33. Fresno, Madera
34. Monterey
35. Orange, San Bernardino
36. San Luis Obispo, Santa Barbara
37. Ventura
38-68. Los Angeles
69-71. Orange
72-73. San Bernardino
74. Riverside
75. Riverside, Imperial
76-80. San Diego

FIGURE 5-3 *Assembly districts, 1966–1971*

traveling on state business. In recent years, legislators have averaged approximately $6,000 annually in allowances, and some have received more than $8,000, in addition to their salaries. The legislature also provides each member with a leased expense-paid car, generous retirement allowances, and death benefits. Moreover, every legislator is provided funds to rent one or more offices in his district, to employ needed administrative assistants and secretaries, and to pay telephone and other office expenses. A few years ago, the state treated its legislators in a niggardly fashion. Now California provides for its legislators as well as any other state and far better than most. On the basis of expenditures per member, the cost of operating the California Legislature is greater than that for any other state.

The legislators

The typical legislator in Sacramento is a college graduate, a member of a number of civic and service organizations, and a prominent person in his community. If he is an assemblyman, he is about forty-eight years old; if a senator, somewhat more than fifty-two. A study of the assembly in 1966 showed that 80 percent of the members had college degrees, 52 percent had professional or graduate degrees, and 25 percent had majored in political science.[4] As Table 5-1 shows, the great majority of California legislators in 1961 to 1969 sessions were businessmen or attorneys. This is to be expected, for persons in these occupations are often well known in their communities and more likely than most other individuals to be able to take time from their employment to campaign for office.

Membership in the senate is generally considered more desirable than in the assembly. The smaller membership adds to the prestige and influence of each individual, and senators also have the advantage of having to run for office only half as often as assemblymen. Partly for these reasons the rate of turnover in membership in the upper house is usually less than in the assembly. However, the number of newly elected

[4] Richard W. Gable and Alexander Cloner, "The California Legislator," in California Constitution Revision Commission, *Proposed Revision of the California Constitution*, Sacramento: State Printing Office, 1966, p. 148.

TABLE 5-1 *Occupations of California legislators*

Senate	1961	1963	1965	1967	1969
Business	13	17	13	11	10
Law	16	12	16	20	20
Agriculture	4	5	3	1	1
Education	1	1	2	4	4
Full-time legislator	1	1	1	2	2
Miscellaneous	5	4	5	2	3
Total	40	40	40	40	40

Assembly	1961	1963	1965	1967	1969
Business	32	26	23	16	18
Law	23	29	31	30	30
Agriculture	5	7	7	10	7
Education	6	9	9	8	6
Full-time legislator	3	2	2	8	10
Miscellaneous	11	7	8	8	9
Total	80	80	80	80	80

SOURCE: *Handbook, California Legislature.* Included as businessmen are those legislators who classify themselves as merchants, contractors, realtors, subdividers, and insurance brokers or agents.

legislators varies widely from one session to another. For example, at the start of the 1969 session there were no senators without previous experience; but in 1970 four were elected to the senate for the first time. Although the turnover in membership in the assembly is higher than in the senate, it, too, varies from one session to another. At the start of the 1965 session, all but ten assemblymen had had prior service in that chamber. In 1971, of the eighty assemblymen, eleven had not had previous assembly service. It should be noted that only a small proportion of those who do not return to the legislature are defeated at the polls. From statehood to 1965 only 86 of the 892 senators who sought reelection were defeated, and only 131 of the 3,055 assemblymen who had sought reelection had been rejected by the voters.[5]

[5] Don A. Allen (ed.), *Legislative Sourcebook*, Sacramento: State Printing Office, 1966, p. 195.

ORGANIZATION OF THE LEGISLATURE

The assembly

THE SPEAKER   The presiding officer of the assembly is the speaker. Because of his functions and prerogatives the speaker is the most important single individual in the legislature and, except for the governor, probably the most influential official in the state. His powers include the following:

1. He appoints the chairman of the Assembly Rules Committee and the chairmen, vice-chairmen, and members of all other assembly standing and special committees.[6]
2. He refers all bills to committees.
3. He recognizes members who wish to speak on the floor of the assembly.
4. He serves as an ex officio member of all assembly committees and joint legislative committees.
5. He votes on all questions and takes part in debates if he so desires.
6. He exercises various other powers as presiding officer, such as keeping order, putting questions to a vote, interpreting the rules, deciding points of order, and signing all acts, resolutions, warrants, and other documents ordered by the assembly.

The speaker, who is elected by the assembly, has invariably been a member of the majority party; but in the past he was usually not first chosen in a party caucus, as is the speaker of the House of Representatives. Instead, members of the majority party in the assembly who wished to become speaker have usually started campaigning for the position months before the legislature convened, soliciting the support of members of both parties by promising chairmanships, vice-chairmanships, and assignments to important committees. It was commonly said that one could determine who voted for the speaker by checking the committee assignments. Political-interest groups and lobbyists interested in the assignment of legislators to specific committees have also at-

---

[6] The governor customarily is permitted to select the chairman of the Assembly Ways and Means Committee, because the chairman of this committee has the responsibility of securing the adoption of the governor's budget.

tempted to gain support for candidates of their choice. Starting in 1968, speakers have been elected by straight party voting. In that year, Jesse M. Unruh was elected speaker with all Democratic assemblymen and no Republicans voting for him, and in 1969 and 1970 Robert Monagan was chosen with all Republican assemblymen and no Democrats supporting him.

Unlike their counterparts in the House of Representatives, most California speakers have held the office for only a short time. Only four persons have been speaker for as long as six years, seven others for four years each, and the remainder for two years or less.[7]

THE RULES COMMITTEE The Assembly Rules Committee handles the administrative affairs of the lower house, performing such functions as assigning offices and desks to assemblymen, selecting secretarial and other employees for the assembly, and approving the expenditure of funds by assembly committees. It consists of the chairman, appointed by the speaker, plus six other members, three from each party, who are first selected in party caucuses and then voted upon by the entire assembly. The chairman, in addition to performing the usual duties of such an office, has the added task of representing the speaker on the committee. No member of either the assembly or senate rules committees may serve as chairman of a standing committee.

OTHER ASSEMBLY OFFICERS The assembly elects a speaker pro tempore to perform the duties of the speaker in case of his absence. He serves ex officio as a member of the rules committee and, in the absence of the chairman, as its chairman.

The speaker appoints from among his supporters a majority floor leader who is the next ranking officer. Traditionally, he serves as the speaker's personal representative on the floor of the assembly rather than as a leader of his party, as do the majority floor leaders in the House and Senate in Washington. Assembly rules provide that the majority floor leader has the duty "to participate in the various debates by making such motions, points of order, or other arrangements as may be necessary to expedite the proceedings of the Assembly, and . . . be

---

[7] Jesse M. Unruh, who served as speaker from 1961 to 1969, held the office longer than any other person.

responsible for the presentation of all matters which relate to the order of business and to the promotion of harmony among the membership."

The minority floor leader is customarily selected by the caucus of the minority party. He serves as the leader of the opposition party and as such plays the role of chief critic of the majority party. He also serves as an ex officio member of the rules committee with full rights of membership except for that of voting.

The senate

THE LIEUTENANT GOVERNOR   The lieutenant governor, who is popularly elected, presides over the senate. His powers are quite limited. They consist only of recognizing members who desire the floor and of deciding points of order. Even on these, however, he may be overruled by a majority of the chamber. He may not introduce bills and he can vote only in case of a tie.

THE PRESIDENT PRO TEMPORE AND THE SENATE RULES COMMITTEE   Far more influential normally than the lieutenant governor is the president pro tempore, who is elected by the senate from among its own members and who performs the duties of the lieutenant governor when he is absent. Although the president pro tempore is the most powerful member of the senate, his opinions seldom carry as much weight as those of the speaker. Partly because the senate is a smaller body, its leadership is less formal and also tends to be shared. Much of the president pro tempore's power is derived from his position as chairman of the Senate Rules Committee, whose other four members, two Republicans and two Democrats, are elected by the senate as a whole. The rules committee has the important functions of appointing the members of all standing committees and of deciding to which committees bills shall be referred.

As was formerly the practice in electing the speaker, the president pro tempore has typically been elected by senators of both parties whose votes are obtained by promises of committee chairmanships and choice committee assignments. For example, after his reelection as president pro tempore in 1969, Hugh Burns reportedly announced that in making committee assignments, "We're going to reward our friends and punish our enemies."[8] Burns, a Democrat, was speaker from 1957 to 1969, although the Democrats did not have a majority in the senate after May, 1967. He was replaced by Republican Howard Way, who was himself displaced by Republican Jack Schrade early in 1970. All three were elected by bipartisan coalitions. Lobbyists and pressure groups have not uncommonly worked to win support for their choice for president pro tempore. For instance, after Schrade's election, one newspaper noted "it was widely reported that lobbyists were working behind the scenes in Schrade's behalf."[9]

Assembly and senate staffs

The California Legislature employs several hundred staff members attached directly to one of the two houses or assigned either to committees or to individual legislators. The rules committee of each house, serving as an executive committee, supervises all of the chief staff members, the most important of which are the chief clerk of the assembly and the secretary of the senate. Each is responsible for the effective functioning of the administrative machinery of the house he serves. Their duties include taking charge of clerical business and printing, seeing that the journals and other records are kept properly, and supervising the work of clerks, stenographers, and pages.

Each assemblyman and senator is allowed from one to three administrative or legislative assistants and one or more secretaries and may when necessary secure additional stenographic help from a typing pool. Since the mid-1960s, the legislature has employed a number of well-qualified staff members referred to as "consultants" or "research specialists" to aid the committees. Today the California Legislature probably has more professionally competent staff assistants than that of any other state.

Standing committees

Like other state legislatures and Congress, the California Legislature makes extensive use of committees. Most important are the standing committees, which handle the bulk of the business during each session.

[8] *Los Angeles Times*, Jan. 12, 1969.
[9] *Los Angeles Times*, Feb. 12, 1970.

Bills and resolutions are customarily referred to a standing committee before being considered by either the assembly or senate as a full body. The subject matter over which the standing committees are given jurisdiction covers all principal areas of state lawmaking, such as agriculture, education, and social welfare. Committees may vary in number and size from one session to the next. During recent sessions, there have been from twenty-one to twenty-five standing committees in the assembly and from fifteen to twenty-two in the senate. The standing committees for 1970 are shown in Table 5-2.

By way of comparison, the United States Senate has sixteen standing committees, and the House of Representatives twenty, supplemented, however, by a considerable number of subcommittees. One reason for the fairly large number of committees in the state is that

TABLE 5-2 *1970 legislative standing committees*

Assembly standing committees		Senate standing committees	
COMMITTEE	NUMBER OF MEMBERS	COMMITTEE	NUMBER OF MEMBERS
Agriculture	11	Agriculture	7
Commerce and Public Utilities	7	Business and Professions	9
Criminal Procedure	7	Education	11
Education	17	Elections and Reapportionment	7
Elections and Constitutional Amendments	13	Finance	13
Finance and Insurance	15	Governmental Organization	13
Government Administration	7	Health and Welfare	11
Governmental Organization	11	Industrial Relations	9
Health and Welfare	13	Insurance and Financial Institutions	9
Intergovernmental Relations	8	Judiciary	13
Judiciary	8	Local Government	11
Labor Relations	7	Natural Resources and Wildlife	9
Local Government	9	Public Utilities and Corporations	5
Natural Resources and Conservation	12	Revenue and Taxation	11
Public Employment and Retirement	8	Rules	5
Revenue and Taxation	15	Transportation	13
Rules	7	Water Resources	9
Transportation	11		
Urban Affairs and Housing	8		
Water	7		
Ways and Means	19		

more legislators can thus share the prestige of being committee chairmen. There is the disadvantage that each legislator is required to serve on too many committees; most assemblymen serve on three committees, and senators serve on as many as five. Another criticism of the California system is that the work load of the committees is unevenly divided. Several of the important committees have large numbers of bills referred to them, while other committees have relatively few.

Staff and auxiliary services

As the problems of the legislature have become more numerous and complicated, California's assemblymen and senators have attempted to improve the process of enacting laws by creating a number of specialized agencies. Among these are the offices of legislative analyst, legislative counsel, and auditor general.

The legislative analyst and his staff provide the legislature with an independent source of information regarding fiscal policies and programs. Their chief responsibilities are to review the budget requests and appropriation bills and to submit recommendations for improving the efficiency of administrative agencies. As one of its main responsibilities, this office prepares for the members of the legislature each year a detailed report entitled *Analysis of the Budget Bill*. This document of some 1,000 pages contains recommendations regarding every item in the governor's budget.

The legislative counsel and his staff in the Legislative Counsel Bureau serve as the legal adviser and the bill-drafting agency of the legislature. This staff drafts the great majority of the bills introduced in the legislature; it prepares a digest of each measure that has been introduced; and it is also authorized to prepare for the governor, at his request, an analysis of any bill that has been passed and sent to him for his approval.

As the title indicates, the principal function of the auditor general and the Legislative Audit Bureau is conducting postaudits of departmental and agency records and accounts. Responsibilities of the bureau include determining that accurate accounts are kept of all financial transactions, that expenditures are made in accordance with applicable laws and regulations, and that agencies account for all funds under their control.

THE LEGISLATIVE PROCESS IN CALIFORNIA

Powers of the legislature

While the principal function of the legislature is the enactment of law, it also possesses other important powers. The powers of the legislature may therefore be classified into two broad categories: (1) legislative, or lawmaking, and (2) nonlawmaking.

LAWMAKING POWERS The California Legislature's lawmaking powers include the following: (1) The legislature controls the public purse. Although the governor takes the lead in preparing the budget, the legislature alone has the power to levy taxes, borrow money, and appropriate funds. (2) The legislature creates all governmental agencies and institutions not provided for by the constitution. (3) It enacts statutes providing for the organization and powers of governing agencies in cities, counties, and other local governmental units. Charter cities and counties have been granted considerable autonomy, but the legislature still has substantial responsibility for many matters pertaining to local communities. (4) It formulates rules and standards that affect such matters of daily life as marriage, divorce, abortion, contracts, deeds, and mortgages. (5) Of major importance are the laws it enacts under the police power regarding public health, safety, morals, and general welfare. Examples of such statutes are laws requiring the licensing and regulating of various professions, trades, and industries; regulating the manufacture and sale of intoxicating liquors; controlling drugs; and authorizing cities and counties to enact ordinances relating to such matters as health, sanitation, zoning, and traffic.

NONLAWMAKING POWERS In addition to enacting statutes, the California Legislature performs from time to time four other important functions.[10] (1) It plays a key role in amending the constitution, and in so doing it exercises a constituent power. (2) The senate, in exercising its

---

[10] The legislature also has the power to impeach state elective officers; but, during the history of the state, impeachment proceedings have been instituted only four times: against a state treasurer, a state controller, and two judges. Only one, the treasurer, was convicted; and this occurred more than a century ago, in 1857.

power to confirm certain of the governor's appointments, performs an executive function. (3) Although prime responsibility for state administration is vested in the governor, the legislature also exercises some administrative powers. Aside from creating administrative agencies, it appropriates funds for their support and may specify their procedures and organization. (4) The power of investigation inheres in the legislature as an essential adjunct to its other powers. Legislative inquiries are usually started by the adoption of a resolution providing for a committee of a single house or a joint committee to investigate some problem situation.

LIMITATIONS ON LEGISLATIVE ACTION   Although the legislature possesses broad authority, its powers are restricted by both the national and state constitutions. Only the limitations contained in the latter will be considered here.

Article I of the California Constitution, entitled the "Declaration of Rights," restricts the legislature in its regulation of persons and property. Included are provisions prohibiting it from abridging freedom of speech, press, or religion; from taking private property for public use without just compensation; and from abolishing jury trials. Actually most of these provisions are unnecessary, for the federal Constitution also prohibits the legislature from enacting measures of these types.

The constitution provides for a variety of other limitations on the power of the legislature. For example, no "special" or "local" statute may be enacted if a general law could serve.[11]

Of considerable importance are the restrictions on the financial powers of the legislature—on its powers of borrowing, taxation, and appropriation. The constitution also imposes restrictions on the organization and procedure of the legislature itself. Provisions of this nature include the requirement that each bill relate to but a single subject, that this subject be expressed in its title, that all amendments to a bill be germane, and that no bill be passable by less than a majority vote of the elected membership of each house. As explained in Chapter 2, the initiative and referendum also constitute restriction on the legislature.

[11] California Constitution, art. IV, sec. 16.

INTRODUCTION AND REFERRAL TO COMMITTEE   The procedure followed by the California Legislature in enacting statutes is similar to that followed by other state legislatures and by Congress (see Figure 5-4).

The first step is the introduction of the bill.[12] Although only senators and assemblymen may introduce bills, most actually originate with other persons or groups—state or local government officials, political-interest groups, or private citizens.[13] Regardless of their origin, most bills are drafted by the staff of the legislative counsel or checked by them before being introduced. (See Figure 5-5.)

Some lawmakers—because of their personalities, political astuteness, bargaining ability, or relationship with powerful pressure groups—have considerably more success than others in obtaining the adoption of legislation. For this reason, lobbyists and organized interests commonly seek out these more influential legislators to "author" or sponsor bills they favor. The author of a bill usually takes the responsibility for "carrying" it, that is, of seeing that it actually moves through the various stages of the legislative process.

COMMITTEE CONSIDERATION AND REPORT   Committee consideration of bills is probably the most important stage of the legislative process. At this time, the thousands of bills are scrutinized; the ones with little support are culled out, and serious consideration is given to those that appear to have merit. As in Congress, a committee chairman greatly influences the fate of a bill by his power to schedule it for a hearing, to preside over the hearings, and to rule on points of parliamentary procedure. Some California committee chairmen have even been able to kill bills favored by a majority of their committee.[14] Much of the bargaining that occurs over a controversial bill may take place between the introduction of a bill and its hearing in committee. During this intervening period, lobbyists often convey to the author the views of the groups they represent. In some instances, lobbyists of groups opposing

---

[12] Proposed laws are known as bills.

[13] One veteran reporter in Sacramento estimated that in California 90 to 95 percent of the bills were originated by persons and groups outside the legislature.

[14] For example, see "Randy Collier: Senate's King of the Road," *Sacramento Bee*, Jan. 26, 1969, p. E-1.

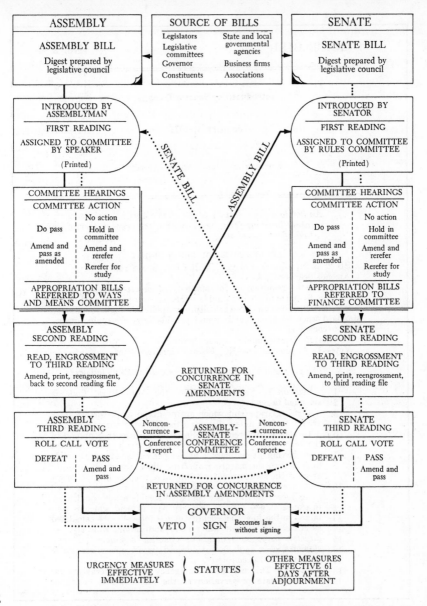

SENATE BILL   No. 2

Introduced by Senator Cologne

January 4, 1971

WITHOUT REFERENCE TO COMMITTEE

An act to amend Section 46867 of the Agricultural Code, re-lating to citrus fruit, and declaring the urgency thereof, to take effect immediately.

LEGISLATIVE COUNSEL'S DIGEST

SB 2, as introduced, Cologne (W.R.T.C.). Grapefruit.

Amends Sec. 46867, Ag.C.

Decreases the requirement for maturity of desert-produced grape-fruit from 6½ parts to 6 parts soluble solids to every part of acid in the juice. Permits Director of Agriculture to establish higher maturity standard when he finds that it would provide more acceptable grape-fruit to consumer.

To take effect immediately, urgency statute.

Vote—⅔; Appropriation—No; Fiscal Committee—Yes.

The people of the State of California do enact as follows:

1   SECTION 1. Section 46867 of the Agricultural Code is
2 amended to read:
3   46867. Grapefruit which are produced in the desert areas
4 are not mature unless they meet the following requirements:
5   In view of differences in climatic conditions that prevail in
6 the desert areas, which result in the grapefruit grown in those
7 areas having, at maturity, a higher percentage of soluble solids
8 to acid than the mature grapefruit which are grown in other
9 areas of the state, grapefruit which are produced in the desert
10 areas are considered mature if at the time of picking and at all
11 times thereafter the juice contains soluble solids equal to or
12 in excess of 6½ 6 parts to every part of acid which is con-
13 tained in the juice. The acidity of the juice shall be calculated
14 as citric acid without water of crystallization. *However, the*
15 *director may, by regulation, establish a higher maturity*
16 *standard when he finds that it would provide a more acceptable*
17 *grapefruit to the consumer.*
18   SEC. 2. This act is an emergency measure necessary for
19 the immediate preservation of the public peace, health or

and favoring a bill compromise their differences and jointly urge amendments to the bill. To avoid opposition from influential groups, the author may decide to accept proposed amendments; and if he does, his amendments will almost always be accepted by the committee. Thus, at times the role of the legislators may resemble that of officials refereeing an athletic match between two opposing teams. Unfortunately, the tendency of legislators to accommodate group demands may at times result in the public interest being overlooked.

Standing committees hold regularly scheduled meetings, which are open to the public unless otherwise determined by the committees. Customarily, the date set for the hearing on a bill is agreed to by the committee chairman and the bill's author. Hearings are usually opened by having the author explain the bill and the reasons why he believes it should be enacted. All persons who wish to testify regarding a bill are usually allowed to present their views. Committee consideration of a crucial bill may continue for hours or even days, whereas hearings on a less important measure will often be brief and amount to no more than a formality.

In the California Legislature the fate of most bills is determined by the committee to which it is assigned. Approximately one-half of the bills introduced die in the standing committee of the house in which they are introduced. Some bills, because of their subject matter, could be referred to one of two or more committees. Whether such a bill reaches the floor of the house may depend upon the composition of the committee to which it is assigned. If the bill goes to a committee favorably disposed to the proposal, it may become a law with little difficulty. On the other hand, if the bill is referred to an unfriendly committee, it may well die there. If an important bill is not "reported out" in due course, it may be discharged from the committee by a majority vote of the total membership of the house concerned, but this is seldom done. Because of this power that committees exercise over bills, the authority to appoint the standing committees and to refer bills to them is of major importance.

FLOOR CONSIDERATION AND PASSAGE   After a committee has considered a bill and has decided to recommend it for passage, the committee reports the measure out to the floor and it is placed on the second reading file. There is usually no opposition to bills at that stage. In most instances, the only serious consideration given a bill on the floor of either house occurs at the time of the third reading.[15] As in the case of the second reading, the bills are seldom read other than by caption or title. Debate on a bill is opened by its sponsor, who explains its scope and purpose. Other legislators may then participate in the debate and offer amendments. In order to pass, a simple majority vote of the membership, that is, twenty-one in the senate and forty-one in the assembly, is required for ordinary legislation but two-thirds is needed for urgency bills, certain finance measures, and constitutional amendments.

If requested by three members, a recorded vote is required on the passage of bills. The senate still uses the voice vote, in which the roll is called alphabetically and the vote of each person is recorded. The assembly has established an electric roll-call system, and the votes are tallied electrically on cards.

Very few bills are killed on the floor of either house. Most bills to which there is strong opposition are blocked in committee or are amended by their authors to make them acceptable. Thus, the great majority of bills passed by the legislature are unopposed on the floor or receive only negligible opposition (see Table 5-3).

Occasionally, identical bills are introduced in both houses and proceed through the two chambers simultaneously. In most cases, however, after a bill has passed one house, it must be transmitted to the other, where the same procedure is followed. If the second house passes the bill without amendment, it goes to the governor for his approval. However, should the second chamber amend the bill, it then requests the first house to accept its amendments. If the first house approves the amended bill, it is promptly enrolled and sent to the governor; if not, it is customarily referred to a conference committee.

CONFERENCE COMMITTEE Conference committees are composed of three members from the assembly and three from the senate. An affirmative vote of at least two members from each house is required for agreement. On some measures, including the state budget, the action of a conference committee is often of major importance. Several meetings

---

[15] Bills that are not revenue measures may be assigned to the consent calendar if they received unanimous approval in committee and encountered no opposition from the membership of the house. Consent calendar bills are voted on without prior debate.

TABLE 5-3   *Action on bills*

	1968			1969		
	ASSEMBLY	SENATE	TOTAL	ASSEMBLY	SENATE	TOTAL
Introduced	2,098	1,276	3,374	2,359	1,433	3,792
Killed in committees	1,031	637	1,668	1,261	727	1,988
Refused passage by assembly or senate	128	45	173	71	36	107
Passed by both houses	939	594	1,533	1,027	671	1,698
Vetoed by governor	36	23	59	41	38	79
Enacted into law	903	571	1,474	986	633	1,619

This summary of action taken on bills by the legislature in the 1968 and 1969 general sessions illustrates the importance of the standing committees. Note the large number of bills killed in the committees and the relatively small number that are defeated at other stages. Volume of legislative business in recent years has exceeded that of any other state legislature. SOURCE: *Final Calendar of Legislative Business,* 1968, 1969.

may be required and much informal bargaining may take place before the members are able to compromise their differences. Lobbyists, officers of organized groups, appointive officials, and other legislators have on occasion attempted to convince members of conference committees to accept or resist particular changes under consideration. After a conference committee files its report, a majority vote by each house is required for its approval. If either house refuses to accept the conference report, another conference committee may be appointed.

ACTION BY THE GOVERNOR   The governor may take any of several courses of action regarding a bill. (1) He may simply sign it, whereupon it becomes a law. (2) If he holds it for twelve days or more while the legislature is in session, it becomes a law without his signature. (3) If during a general session the legislature adjourns before twelve days have expired and the governor neither signs nor vetoes the bill, it then becomes a law at the end of thirty days. (4) The governor may veto the bill and return it to the house of origin with a statement explaining his objections. Before vetoing a measure, governors have customarily consulted with legislative leaders and with spokesmen for organized interest groups especially concerned with the measure. The legislature may override a veto by a two-thirds vote of the members of each house; however, this has not occurred since 1946.

In 1966, the electorate approved a constitutional amendment providing that thirty days after the end of a general session the legislature should reconvene for not more than five days to reconsider bills vetoed by the governor since the adjournment of the legislature.[16] No attempt to override a veto has come close to succeeding in these sessions; as a result, many legislators have suggested that it be abolished.

The item veto is a power granted to the governor of California that is not given to the President of the United States. If an appropriation bill contains several items, the governor may reduce or eliminate any item while approving the remainder. He can do this by appending to the bill at the time he signs it a statement listing the items to which he objects and his reason for vetoing them. If the legislature is in session, he sends a copy of his veto statement to the house in which the bill originated. The legislature may, of course, override the veto.

Acts providing for elections or appropriating funds for current state expenses, tax levies, or emergency measures take effect at once. All other acts take effect sixty-one days after the adjournment of a regular session. This delay provides an opportunity for the filing of referendum petitions to prevent laws from taking effect until voted upon by the electorate.

Political parties and the legislature

Political parties have never played as major a role in the legislative process in California as they have in Congress or in many other states. A former secretary of the senate observed: "Roll calls in the two houses of the Legislature follow different alignments on nearly every issue, with Democratic and Republican votes on each side. . . . On rare occasions some question arises which calls for a vote on political lines, but . . . very few roll calls have been discovered wherein all the Republicans have voted on one side and all the Democrats on the other."[17]

There are several reasons why party organization in the legislature has been weak and why divisions of votes along party lines have not been frequent. (1) Political parties in California have not been highly

[16] Previously, if the legislature adjourned before ten days expired, all bills not signed at the end of thirty days were "pocket vetoed."
[17] Joseph A. Beek, *The California Legislature*, Sacramento: State Printing Office, 1965, p. 153.

organized or disciplined. (2) North-south and rural-urban cleavages have at times been important factors in voting on legislative issues. (3) In some instances, organized economic interests, or pressure groups, have been more influential than party affiliation in determining a legislator's vote. (4) In running for office many legislators have sought the votes of people in both parties and thus hesitate to take partisan stands that might alienate a bloc of their constituents.

It is interesting to note that the seating arrangement of California's legislators is not on a partisan basis, as it is in Congress. Seats are rather assigned according to seniority and without regard to political affiliation. Also, unlike Congress where the standing committees usually reflect the strength of the two parties and are invariably chaired by members of the majority party, in California it is not uncommon for members of the minority party to outnumber the majority party on some committees or to be chosen as committee chairmen.[18]

Since the early 1960s, however, the California Legislature has become increasingly partisan due largely to attempts by both parties to strengthen their organizations throughout the state, to the end of cross-filing, and to efforts of Governor Edmund G. "Pat" Brown and Governor Ronald Reagan to utilize partisan majorities in the assembly and senate to secure the enactment of their legislative programs. Voting along party lines increases in each house when the budget and tax measures are being considered. Issues like education, labor, and social welfare also tend to divide members along party lines. In recent years, as in times past, political parties have exerted more influence on voting in the assembly than in the senate. The upper house has been described as having a "clubby atmosphere where a man's party counts for less than his seniority and his ability to get along."[19] Both parties in the assembly have held weekly caucuses during legislative sessions for several years, but regular caucuses were not initiated in the senate until 1967.

As noted earlier, since 1968 the speaker has been selected by a straight party vote, but the election of the president pro tempore of

[18] For example, in 1967 with the Democrats outnumbering the Republicans 21 to 19 in the senate and 42 to 38 in the assembly, ten Republicans in the upper house and eleven in the assembly were selected as chairmen of committees; and in 1970 with the Republicans controlling the senate 21 to 19 and the assembly 41 to 39, Democrats were chairmen of six senate committees and seven assembly committees.

[19] *California Journal*, vol. 1, no. 2, p. 35, February, 1970.

the senate has continued on a bipartisan basis. Somewhat to the surprise of most political observers, the bipartisan "old guard" clique continued to dominate the senate after reapportionment in 1965. This was accomplished in part by emphasizing seniority in making committee assignments. However, with the retirement of several of these older senators in 1970, new leaders are expected to emerge; and political parties are likely to play a greater role in the senate as well as in the assembly.

Legislative reforms

Both the reputation and the performance of the California Legislature have improved during recent years; however, a number of additional reforms are needed. The legislative process would undoubtedly be improved if the "lobby law" were amended to require the submission of additional information concerning lobbyists and organized pressure groups, if more meaningful conflict-of-interest laws were enacted, and if a more adequate corrupt practices act were adopted to require each legislator to make a complete disclosure of the sources of his campaign funds and how they are spent. There should also be a reduction in the number of standing committees and an equalization of their work loads. Consideration might well be given, too, to the creation of joint standing committees. If, instead of having separate sets of committees in each house, a joint committee system were adopted, there would be one series of committees each with members from both houses. This should save both time and money. Joint committees have proven successful in Massachusetts, Maine, and Connecticut. Why not try the idea in California?

On one of the state buildings in Sacramento are inscribed the words: "Give me men to match my mountains." Possibly more now than at any other time in the past, California needs legislators of such stature. Many California legislators have been men of outstanding ability and integrity, but the increased complexity of legislative work demands state lawmakers more able and informed than some who have served. Legislators should be persons qualified by experience, education, and temperament to take a broad, balanced view of public questions, people capable of weighing opposing arguments and interests and able to reach decisions in which the public interest is paramount.

CHAPTER 6

𝒯HE EXECUTIVE

In California and most other states, executive power is not completely consolidated in the chief executive as it is in the national government, in which only the President and Vice President are elected and all other executive officials are appointed by the President. The California electorate chooses not only the governor and lieutenant governor, but also the attorney general, controller, secretary of state, treasurer, superintendent of public instruction, and the four elective members of the Board of Equalization. Thus California has not one but eleven top executives, each elected directly by the people and authorized by the state constitution and statutes to perform particular functions.

THE GOVERNOR

Compensations and qualifications

The governor, who is vested by the constitution with "the supreme executive power," is the most important and influential of the state officials. He receives an annual salary of $49,100, more than the governor of any other state except New York. Other allowances and perquisites include a limousine with a chauffeur, and funds for house rental, travel, entertainment, and staff assistance.

The governor must be a citizen of the United States and must also have been a resident of the state for at least five years before his election. He takes office on the first Monday after the first day of January following his election and may be removed before the expiration of his term either by impeachment and conviction or through a recall. There is no limit on the number of terms he may serve. Earl Warren, who was elected three times, was the only governor to be elected more than twice, and only three other governors have been elected to two 4-year terms—Hiram Johnson in 1910 and 1914, Edmund G. Brown in 1958 and 1962, and Ronald Reagan in 1966 and 1970. Three lieutenant governors who have succeeded to the gubernatorial office upon the death or resignation of an incumbent have subsequently been elected governor. All other governors have held the office for four years or less.

The state legislature has established a line of succession to the governorship and a method of replacing a governor who becomes disabled. The lieutenant governor is first in line of succession to the office, followed by the senate president pro tempore, the assembly speaker, secretary of state, attorney general, treasurer, and controller. The legislature has also provided for a Commission on the Governorship, which is vested with the authority to petition the state supreme court to decide any question of a governor's disability.[1]

---

[1] The commission is composed of the senate president pro tempore, the assembly speaker, the president of the University of California, the chancellor of the California state colleges, and the state director of finance.

The governor's staff

The governor and his staff occupy a suite on the first floor of the capitol. The size and organization of the staff vary according to the particular governor and his method of working. The staff has grown over the years; and during Reagan's administration it has included some twenty-five staff secretaries, staff assistants and administrative and special assistants. In addition to these top assistants, the governor has a personal secretary, an office supervisor, receptionists, and approximately sixty stenographers and clerks.

The staff secretaries and the other top administrative aides have a variety of tasks. Some perform specialized functions. The executive secretary serves as a kind of chief of staff, directing and coordinating the work of others and supervising the general operation of the governor's office. Other principal aides in recent years have included a cabinet secretary who maintains liaison with the state agencies, a press secretary and an assistant press secretary whose duties include preparing news releases and arranging press conferences and radio and television broadcasts, an appointments secretary who maintains a record of the positions to be filled and makes recommendations to the governor regarding possible appointees for them, a legal affairs secretary whose principal responsibility is advising the governor on executive clemency and extradition processes, and a legislative secretary who serves as liaison with the legislature. Typically, several members of the governor's staff have such assignments as investigating or making studies of particular problems, planning and coordinating programs, and writing speeches for the governor.[2] Because the governor relies on their judgment and is in daily contact with them, these gubernatorial assistants have strong influence on his decisions and policies. The importance the governor attaches to these key assistants is indicated in part by their salaries. On the recommendation of Governor Reagan, the legislature in 1969 increased the annual salary of the executive secretary to $35,000, and provided for other staff secretaries and administrative assistants to receive from $20,000 to $27,000.

[2] Individuals performing such tasks have had various titles; one of Reagan's aides was called the planning and research director and another the program development section chief.

POWERS AND RESPONSIBILITIES OF GOVERNOR

As chief executive of the state, the governor occupies a position some-what similar to that of the President in the national government. Indeed, because of the size of the state, its rapid growth, and the complexity of its many problems, the office of the governor of California is perhaps as difficult as any other executive office in the United States other than that of President.

Civic and political leadership

Responsible leadership is indispensable to the successful operation of any form of government. The governor, as the principal elective official, is to most citizens the symbol of the unity and authority of the state and is expected to represent the public interest against the divisive aims of special interests. The fact that Governor Reagan has received on an average more than 320,000 letters each year is some indication of the extent to which the people look to the governor for leadership.

As civic leader or "chief of state," the governor engages in various activities of a ceremonial nature. Visiting dignitaries from other states and from foreign countries are greeted by the governor. He is invited to lay cornerstones for new buildings, to cut ribbons opening freeways, and to deliver addresses at celebrations, conventions, and innumerable other public and private functions.[3] These ceremonial activities are a heavy drain on the governor's energy and consume time that he might otherwise devote to more important gubernatorial responsibilities, but the public considers them a part of the governor's job.

Upon his election, the governor becomes the titular head of his party in the state. In this capacity, he is able to influence the choice of certain party officials. He is expected to attend and to address party meetings and rallies, to participate actively in campaigns to elect candidates to national and state offices, and to aid his party in various other ways. Customarily, he heads his party's delegation to its national convention. Like the governor of New York, the chief executive of California, upon his election, almost automatically becomes a potential candidate for the presidency.

[3] For example, Governor Reagan has received an average of six hundred invitations a month, most of them involving speeches.

The governor's various responsibilities force him to assume dual roles. In most instances, to obtain his party's nomination, the governor must have been active in politics; and, after his election, he is expected to lead his party and to work for its success. Although he naturally serves as the leader of his party, it is assumed that he will at the same time be the nonpartisan champion of all the people. In brief, the governor is expected simultaneously to be both a partisan and a nonpartisan leader. Most governors have attempted to solve this dilemma by administering the state's official business in a genuinely nonpartisan way while reserving exhibitions of partisanship for strictly party functions.

The governor as chief legislator

During the past few decades, the people of California have come more and more to look to the governor for leadership in the formulation of public policy. The role of legislative leader has devolved on him out of necessity; he is the only person in the state who has the facilities to develop comprehensive statewide programs and whose position enables him to organize sufficient support from the public and among the members of the legislature to secure their adoption. To a large extent, the reputation of a governor today is built upon his policies, which collectively comprise his administration's program.

With respect to the legislature, the governor possesses a number of powers that give him considerable strength in policy making. Some of these are specifically defined in the state constitution, while others have grown out of the combination of popular demand and the practices of the state's more energetic and able governors. The extent to which a governor may successfully utilize these powers depends, however, upon a number of circumstances, including his ability and personality, the political composition of the legislature during his term, and the nature of the problems then confronting the state.

LEGISLATION MESSAGES AND RECOMMENDATIONS The constitution states that the governor shall deliver to the legislature each year an address on "the condition of the state" and that he may recommend legislation accordingly. In his opening message, he usually outlines his legislative program. During a session he ordinarily delivers—either in person or in writing—several other messages, elaborating on his initial recommendations or adding others.

The authority to recommend legislation implies certain other powers. Often bills designed to carry out the principal parts of the governor's program are drafted at his request by his staff or by the legislative counsel and are given to influential legislators to introduce. Proposals introduced at the governor's request are customarily referred to as "administration bills," and during Governor Brown's administration the practice was started of labeling such bills with the notation "By request of the Governor." As a large number of important bills originate in the executive departments, the governor, through his control over departmental bills, may exert considerable influence on legislative action.

BUDGETARY POWERS   Although the process of preparing the state budget will be discussed later in the chapter, it should be noted here that by law as well as custom the California governor is the chief legislator in budgetary matters. He is responsible for planning the state's expenditures and for recommending measures to provide the necessary funds. The legislature may, of course, amend the governor's budget, but in most years the budget approved by the legislature has closely approximated that submitted by the governor.

The governor's budgetary powers enable him to bargain quite effectively with individual senators and assemblymen for their cooperation. The legislature is required to act on the budget before considering any other appropriation bill except measures providing for legislative expenses or bills designated by the governor as emergency measures. Needless to say, a legislator who has supported the governor's program will usually have less difficulty in getting an emergency designation for a bill of importance to his district than one who has not.

VETO POWER   The governor participates directly in the legislative process through his power to approve or veto legislation. Vetoes in California are of two types—the general veto and the item veto.[4] They may be overridden by a two-thirds vote of each house, but this rarely occurs.

A general veto rejects the entire bill. In some instances, governors

---

[4] Before 1967, governors made effective use of the pocket veto, which permitted them to kill any bill that reached their desk during the final ten days of the legislative session by simply not signing it. The pocket veto no longer applies to bills passed by the legislature in a general session.

have forestalled the enactment of particular bills simply by making an early announcement that they would be vetoed if passed.

The item veto allows the governor to delete or reduce specific items in an appropriation bill without rejecting the entire measure. This power is especially significant in enabling a governor to obtain the adoption of his budget without being required to approve expenditures that he believes to be unsound.

As one observer of the California legislative process has written, the governor's veto power is "a weapon which has been used to wring from legislators reluctant votes in behalf of his program."[5] On occasion, legislators have voted for administration bills in the belief that the governor would reward their support by not vetoing measures of particular interest to them and their constituents. It should be noted that governors have not used the veto power irresponsibly and have not vetoed bills simply to punish their authors. In an average session, less than 5 percent of the bills passed by the legislature are vetoed, and these are seldom of major importance. For instance, of the 1,705 bills passed by the legislature in 1970, Governor Reagan vetoed only 77.

SPECIAL SESSIONS If he deems it necessary, the governor may call the legislature into special session, during which it may act only on the subject or subjects specified in the call. Since the adoption of annual general sessions of the legislature, there has been little need for special sessions and few have been called. The constitution also grants the governor the relatively unimportant power of adjourning the legislature if the two houses cannot agree on a time.

EXTRACONSTITUTIONAL POWERS Some of the governor's powers are not mentioned in the constitution but have developed in response to needs. His success in working with legislators may depend to a considerable extent on his utilization of these powers. If the governor's office and both houses of the legislature are controlled by the same political party, he may make effective use of his position as party leader to gain support for his program. Some chief executives have exerted influence in the choice of the speaker, other legislative officials, and committee chairmen.

[5] Joseph A. Beek, *The California Legislature*, Sacramento: California State Printing Office, 1965, p. 106.

During legislative sessions, some governors have met regularly with the leaders of their party in the assembly and senate to discuss policies and plan strategy to follow in securing the enactment of agreed-upon policies. In such meetings and at other times as well, legislators belonging to the governor's party are urged to support the administration's program in order to strengthen the position of the party in the state.

Most governors, realizing that they must have backing from legislators of both parties in order to secure the enactment of certain measures, have attempted to cultivate good relations with all legislators. Their techniques include individual conferences with the legislators, small group luncheons, and dinner parties for legislators and their wives. Ordinarily, however, a governor's persuasiveness with legislators depends on more than friendly gestures or sheer logic; he must convince them that he has the ability and determination to make full use of the advantages that are his because of his office and authority.

Recent governors have assigned to specific staff assistants the special task of coordinating the administration's legislative program and serving as liaison with the legislature. The legislative secretary and other members of the governor's staff work closely with the assemblymen and senators carrying administration bills—assisting sponsors in preparing information for committee hearings, arranging for witnesses, and talking to committee members and other legislators in somewhat the same fashion as lobbyists. Members of the governor's staff also analyze all other bills to determine which ones he should support or oppose.

Although most positions in California state government are filled through competitive civil service examinations, the governor's power of appointment continues to be important. Most governors use this patronage to build legislative support as well as to pay political debts.

One of the governor's most important sources of strength is his ability to influence public opinion. As the chief executive, his every action or pronouncement is publicized in newspapers throughout the state. No other person in California commands this attention. The governor can focus public attention on his legislative program in his weekly press conferences, in news releases prepared by his press secretary, and in other public statements and addresses. If he is skilled at public relations, he may also be able to bring pressure to bear on the legislature by appealing directly to the electorate. Governor Reagan, with many years of experience as a motion picture and television performer, has found television a particularly effective medium for appealing to the public. Many of his press conferences have been filmed for later showing on television. Occasionally, he has previewed state budgets and other proposals on television before submitting them to the legislature, and he periodically makes televised reports on one phase or another of state government. In addition, Governor Reagan has filmed a number of short statements which could be shown on the regular television news programs.

Executive and administrative powers and responsibilities

ADMINISTRATIVE SUPERVISION As the chief executive, the governor is responsible for directing and coordinating the administrative agencies of the state; but, for three practical reasons, it is difficult for him to do so. (1) As has been noted, several other executive officers are elected directly by the voters and are therefore not accountable to him. (2) Some state services are performed by administrative and policy-making boards, many of which function with considerable freedom from executive control. (3) The sheer number of agencies makes it virtually impossible for any one individual to exercise effective supervision over all of them.

In 1961, Governor Brown undertook the first major reorganization of the executive branch of the California state government in more than thirty years. The reorganization plan provided for the establishment of eight major agencies under which would be placed all executive departments, boards, and commissions, except those headed by constitutional officers. In 1968, the legislature approved a proposal of Governor Reagan for further reorganization of the executive branch (except for departments headed by elected officials) into four major agencies: Business and Transportation, Resources, Human Relations, and Agriculture and Services (see Figure 6-1).

One of the principal purposes of the reorganization was to enable the governor to coordinate, control, and plan more effectively the various programs and functions within the executive branch.

THE CABINET In addition to supervising the work of the administrative units within his agency, each of the four major agency heads also serves

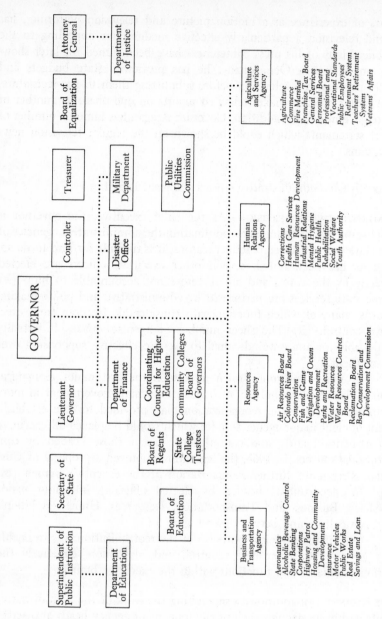

FIGURE 6-1 Organization of the executive branch of California state government

GOVERNOR

Superintendent of Public Instruction — Department of Education

Secretary of State

Lieutenant Governor — Department of Finance

Controller

Treasurer — Military Department — Disaster Office

Board of Equalization

Attorney General — Department of Justice

Board of Education

Board of Regents / State College Trustees

Coordinating Council for Higher Education / Community Colleges Board of Governors

Public Utilities Commission

Business and Transportation Agency
Aeronautics
Alcoholic Beverage Control
State Banking
Corporations
Highway Patrol
Housing and Community Development
Insurance
Motor Vehicles
Public Works
Real Estate
Savings and Loan

Resources Agency
Air Resources Board
Colorado River Board
Conservation
Fish and Game
Navigation and Ocean Development
Parks and Recreation
Water Resources
Water Resources Control Board
Reclamation Board
Bay Conservation and Development Commission

Human Relations Agency
Corrections
Health Care Services
Human Resources Development
Industrial Relations
Mental Hygiene
Public Health
Rehabilitation
Social Welfare
Youth Authority

Agriculture and Services Agency
Agriculture
Commerce
Fire Marshal
Franchise Tax Board
General Services
Personnel Board
Professional and Vocational Standards
Public Employees' Retirement System
Teachers' Retirement System
Veterans' Affairs

as a member of the governor's cabinet. Other persons attending the cabinet meetings include the lieutenant governor, the attorney general, the superintendent of public instruction, the head of the Coordinating Council for Higher Education, the director of finance, and members of the governor's immediate staff. The cabinet usually meets with the governor biweekly to advise him on state problems, to assist him in formulating state policies, and to coordinate their execution.

APPOINTIVE POWERS The governor has extensive powers of appointment, although certain executive officers are elected and the great majority of state employees are selected on the basis of competitive civil service examinations. Except for the other elective executives, the governor appoints all of the state's top administrators. In addition to the heads of four major agencies, these include the directors and deputy directors of such departments as Highway Patrol, Social Welfare, Public Health, Fish and Game, and others (see Figure 6-1). The governor also appoints the members of various boards and commissions serving on a full-time basis. These include, among others, the Public Utilities Commission and the State Personnel Board. These appointees (approximately 150) together with the governor's personal staff, constitute his most important appointments from the standpoint of the operation of the state government. Indeed, through them, a governor can do a great deal to determine the character and quality of his administration and his reputation as an executive.

The governor also makes a large number of appointments to boards and commissions whose members serve on a part-time basis. These include such diverse organizations as the Horse Racing Board, the Historical Landmark Advisory Committee, the Board of Regents of the University of California, the Industrial Welfare Commission, and the district agricultural board found in most of California's counties. There are now more than 1,400 such positions; but, since members of these boards frequently have overlapping terms some of which are longer than four years, a governor often is unable in one term to change the membership of a board completely. Partly for this reason he can exercise relatively little influence over the activities of most boards. Persons holding these part-time positions are usually paid no more than expenses, but because of their prestige, these positions are highly desired and constitute an important part of the governor's patronage.

In addition to these appointments, governors may fill vacancies occurring in state, county, or municipal courts, in other state elective executive offices, on county boards of supervisors, or in either of California's two United States Senate seats. Appointees to these vacancies hold office, however, only until the succeeding general election.

Perhaps the governor's power to fill vacancies on the bench due to retirement, death, or resignation of incumbents and to appoint judges to newly created judicial positions constitutes his most important patronage power.[6] There is a sizable number of these positions and they are the most highly sought-after political prizes in the state. Judges receive good salaries, have high prestige, and usually have no difficulty in getting reelected until they choose to retire on generous pensions. Since many legislators who are attorneys wish judgeships, the governor's power to make these appointments is an important factor in his ability to secure legislative support for his program. On the average, a governor appoints seventy to eighty judges a year.

To find qualified persons for these various positions, the governor's appointments secretary develops files on prospective appointees; and the governor seeks recommendations from party leaders, friends, and other influential persons throughout the state. Most governors have consistently appointed members of the opposing party as well as their own.

FINANCIAL CONTROLS The executive budget provides the governor with a powerful instrument of administrative control as well as with a means for exerting legislative leadership. Through the budget he passes upon the programs of administrative agencies and controls their expenditures. As executive and administrative officials must obtain the governor's approval of their proposed expenditures, they are inclined to follow his leadership and to cooperate with his general program. Much of the governor's budgetary power is exercised through the Department of Finance, which has general supervision over the state's financial activities and serves as his principal staff agency.

After the legislature approves the budget, the Finance Department has the responsibility of supervising its execution. It maintains continuous supervision over expenditures to see that they are consistent with

---

[6] In his first three years in office, Governor Reagan appointed 238 judges.

the governor's overall program, are authorized by law, and do not exceed the amounts appropriated.

The Department of Finance assists the governor in various other ways to coordinate and control the state's administrative system. Among these ways are (1) conducting management surveys of state agencies and making recommendations for improving their organization and procedures, (2) approving state contracts and other financial transactions, and (3) determining and adjusting salaries for certain positions exempt from the civil service system. In addition, one division of the department has the responsibility of coordinating the state's building construction program; it approves the plans, allocates funds, and determines the timing of the major construction projects of each state agency.

RELATIONS WITH NATIONAL GOVERNMENT AND OTHER STATES Included among the governor's extensive executive and administrative duties and powers is his responsibility for representing the state in its relations with the national government and with other states. To find solutions to problems involving California and the national government, the governor may confer with the President or testify before congressional committees. From time to time, the governor will meet with the chief executives of adjoining states, and he usually attends the annual Governors' Conference, which is held to permit the chief executives of all the states to discuss problems of mutual concern.

The governor's leading role in interstate relations may be illustrated by noting the part he plays in the extradition of fugitives from justice. Before a person may be extradited from California, the governor must sign the extradition papers and request the attorney general and the district attorney of the county in which the fugitive is located to assist in the extradition. To secure the return of a person who has fled from California, the governor must request the chief executive of the state in which the fugitive is located to extradite him.

Judicial powers

The California governor performs certain duties of a judicial or quasi-judicial nature. As has been noted, he is authorized to make certain appointments to the judiciary when vacancies occur between elections or when new judgeships are created. Other than that, his most important judicial power is his authority to grant reprieves, commutations, and pardons to persons who have been convicted of crimes. A reprieve is a temporary postponement of punishment, a commutation is a reduction in the punishment, and a pardon is a relatively complete release from penalty.

The governor's pardoning power does not apply to federal offenses and to certain state offenses. He may not act in cases of impeachment, and if a convict has been twice convicted of a felony, the governor may not grant a pardon or commutation unless recommended by the state supreme court. At the beginning of each legislative session, the governor must issue a report listing every case of executive clemency.

Recent governors have assigned one of their top assistants the task of investigating and reporting to them on applications for executive clemency. Customarily, information upon which to render clemency decisions is sought from the Adult Authority, the Board of Trustees of the California Institution for Women, the attorney general, and the courts. The governor, however, must make the final decision.

Military and emergency powers

The governor is the commander in chief of the state military forces. Thus he is the military, as well as the civil, head of the state. The constitution authorizes him to call out the National Guard to execute the laws of the state and to suppress riots or domestic disturbances. As the National Guard is part of the armed forces of the United States, it is under the jurisdiction of both the state and the national government. The immediate head of the National Guard is the adjutant general, who is appointed by the governor with the approval of the President.

The governor's emergency powers have been amplified due to the possibility of enemy attack. The Civil Defense Act, adopted in the 1950s, granted the governor additional emergency powers and created the state Disaster Council and the California Disaster Office. The governor is given the responsibility of developing a state civil defense and disaster plan and is empowered to proclaim under certain conditions a "state of extreme emergency" or a "state of disaster."

CONSTITUTIONAL OFFICERS

The lieutenant governor, attorney general, secretary of state, controller, treasurer, superintendent of public instruction, and four members of the Board of Equalization—like the governor—are elected for four-year terms in the even-numbered years between presidential elections. The annual salaries of these officials range from $25,000 paid each member of the Board of Equalization, to $35,000 received by the attorney general. The lieutenant governor, controller, treasurer, secretary of state, and superintendent of public instruction are paid $30,000 each. As these officials and many of their duties are specifically provided for in the state constitution, they are termed constitutional officers.

Early in the state's history, a large share of the administrative activities of the state was performed by these officials and their subordinates. As other administrative activities were undertaken by the state, new agencies were created and provision was made for their heads to be appointed by the governor. Today there is little distinction between the type of functions performed by the constitutional officials and the type performed by administrative officials appointed by the governor. For this reason and because of the desirability of coordinating the various units of the executive branch under unified leadership, many students of state government have urged a reduction in the number of state elective executive officers. Some states, especially those with newer constitutions, have followed that advice and provide for the voters to elect only one or two executive officers. The voters elect only the governor and lieutenant governor in Hawaii and the governor and secretary of state in Alaska.

The lieutenant governor

California and all but eleven of the other states have created the position of lieutenant governor to provide a reserve chief executive in case the governor became unable to continue in office. If the governor resigns, dies, becomes permanently incapacitated, or is impeached and convicted, the lieutenant governor becomes the chief executive. If the governor is temporarily absent from the state or becomes too ill to continue in office, the lieutenant governor may exercise the functions of the office until the governor is able to resume his responsibilities. The qualifications of the position are the same as those for governor. Unlike candidates for Vice President of the United States, who are selected by their party's candidate for the presidency, the lieutenant governor in California is nominated and elected separately. Hence, although the state's governor and lieutenant governor have always been from the same party, it would be possible for them to be from opposite parties.

The lieutenant governor serves as the president of the senate, but his legislative powers are limited to presiding over the upper house and voting in case of a tie. The lieutenant governor may, however, exercise some power informally in the senate through his personal influence. The lieutenant governor is a member of several boards and commissions, including the Board of Regents of the University of California; the Board of Trustees of the State Colleges; the Commission on Interstate Cooperation; and the State Lands Commission, which has jurisdiction over all state-owned land, including some 3 million acres of tideland. Ed Reinecke, who was elected lieutenant governor in 1970, was first appointed to that position in 1969 when President Nixon selected his predecessor, Robert Finch, as Secretary of Health, Education and Welfare.

The attorney general

The attorney general is the second most important elected executive official in the state. He heads the Department of Justice and is the state's chief legal officer. The duties of the attorney general may be grouped into four categories. First, along with the governor, he is responsible for seeing that state laws are enforced. As the state's "chief law officer" he may supervise the work of the district attorneys, sheriffs, and other law enforcement officers and, when requested, assist local law enforcement officials in the apprehension and prosecution of criminals. If any state law is not being properly enforced in any county, he has the authority to assume the powers of district attorney and to prosecute any law violations. His actions as attorney general set the tone for law enforcement in the entire state.

Second, the attorney general serves as legal adviser to the governor, other administrative officers and agencies, the state legislature, and local government agencies. He gives legal advice to the governor concerning bills awaiting his signature and prepares formal opinions regarding the meaning and interpretation of state laws. This is an important power, for these opinions, which are published periodically, are considered the official interpretation of the law unless reversed by court decisions. In addition, members of his staff often informally advise state and county officials through personal conferences and correspondence.

Third, the attorney general represents the state in cases in which it sues or is sued. During the course of a year the office of the attorney general handles numerous civil and criminal cases. Most of the criminal cases involve appeals from convictions in cases tried in the lower courts.

Finally, the attorney general serves as a member of a number of boards and commissions. The position of attorney general was a stepping stone to the gubernatorial office for both Earl Warren and Edmund G. "Pat" Brown. The present attorney general, Evelle J. Younger, was elected in 1970.

The controller

The controller is the state's principal accounting and disbursing officer. As such he maintains its central control accounts, including complete records of all receipts, payments, and balances in the state treasury. He audits all claims for payment from state funds; no disbursements may be made from the treasury except on warrants approved by his office. In part, these functions of the controller duplicate those of the director of finance; and, because of this duplication, several proposals have been made for abolishing the office or for a general reorganization that would transfer certain functions to other agencies. The controller also supervises the work of county fiscal officials. He prescribes the financial forms that they use and the rules and regulations that they follow in performing their functions.

The office of the controller is an important tax-collecting agency of the state. The controller is chairman of the Franchise Tax Board, which is responsible for the state income tax and the corporation tax; and he is a member of the Board of Equalization, which administers the sales, use, and gasoline taxes. His office is also responsible for collecting inheritance and gift taxes, the insurance company tax, motor fuel taxes, and several other types of taxes as well. The controller appoints the inheritance tax appraisers in each of the fifty-eight counties. As these appointments are commonly considered to be political patronage and a potential source of support for the incumbent controller at election time, bills have been introduced in recent legislative sessions to place these positions under civil service. In addition to the two boards mentioned above, the controller serves on several other boards and commissions. The present controller, Houston Flournoy, was elected in 1966, and reelected in 1970.

The secretary of state

The secretary of state is commonly referred to as the state's chief clerk. He is the custodian of state documents, including all acts passed by the legislature, reports and records of administrative agencies and legislative committees, and the state seal, which he uses to authenticate state documents. In addition, he registers trademarks and issues certificates of incorporation. Before any corporation may conduct business in California, its articles of incorporation must be approved and filed in his office. As was noted in Chapter 3, the secretary of state is also the chief election officer of the state.

From 1910 until 1970, only two men—a father and son—had been elected secretary of state. Frank C. Jordan was elected in 1910 and held the office until his death in 1940, when Paul Peek was appointed to complete the term. In 1942 Frank M. Jordan—who had served as an assistant to his father—was elected and was then reelected every four years until he died in 1970. In 1970, Edmund G. Brown, Jr., the son of former Governor Edmund G. Brown, was elected secretary of state.

The treasurer

The treasurer is the official custodian of state funds and securities. He provides a banking service for state agencies by receiving all state revenues, keeping them safely, and paying them out on vouchers or warrants signed by the controller. The treasurer is required to keep records of all moneys received and paid out and to submit reports periodically to the governor, controller, and state legislature. The funds received by him are deposited in banks throughout the state, from which payments are made. Surplus funds are invested by the treasurer in government securities or deposited in bank accounts that will draw interest. The treasurer is also responsible for the sale and redemption of and the payment of interest on state bonds.

As the duties of the office are not of a policy-making nature, there appears to be little reason for electing the treasurer, and in 1959 the Committee on Reorganization of California State Government recommended that the office of treasurer be abolished and its duties be transferred to other agencies.

Mrs. Ivy Baker Priest, who had served as United States treasurer under President Dwight Eisenhower, was elected state treasurer in 1966 and was reelected in 1970.

Superintendent of public instruction

The superintendent of public instruction is the only state executive who is elected on a nonpartisan ballot. He serves as the director of the Department of Education and the secretary and executive officer of the state Board of Education appointed by the governor. This board, in turn, is designated as the governing and policy-determining body of the Department of Education. Thus the superintendent of public instruction, an independently elected officer, is in the anomalous position of heading a state department whose policies are determined by an appointive board.

As head of the Department of Education, the superintendent regulates and provides professional assistance to all publicly supported schools and colleges of the state except the University of California and the state colleges. He serves ex officio as a member of the Board of Regents of the University of California and of the Board of Trustees of the state colleges. Wilson Riles, the present superintendent, was elected to this office in 1970.

The Board of Equalization

The Board of Equalization is the principal tax agency of the state. It consists of the controller, who serves as an ex officio member, and four full-time members, who are elected for four-year terms by district. Each full-time member is responsible for administering the activities of the board in his district.

The board received its name from its basic function of equalizing property tax assessments among the fifty-eight counties of the state. The importance of this function today may be seen by noting that millions of dollars of state funds are annually distributed to local governments according to formulas based on assessed property values. The board's other duties relating to the assessment of property include prescribing rules for local assessors and assisting them with their duties, assessing public utility property for purposes of local taxation, and assessing insurance companies and other businesses that are taxed by the state government. At present, one of the major activities of the Board of Equalization is the collection of taxes. Approximately two-thirds of the state's revenue is derived from taxes administered by the board. Among these are the gasoline and diesel fuel taxes, the retail sales and use taxes, insurance company tax, alcoholic beverages taxes, and the highway users tax on trucks and buses.

STATE PERSONNEL AND FINANCE

As California has the largest population of all the states, it naturally has more state employees and a higher budget than any other state. More than 180,000 employees and an annual expenditure of nearly 7 billion dollars are now required to operate the government of California. As long as the population keeps on growing and government services continue to expand, more state employees and increased expenditures must be expected.

Personnel

Much of California's reputation for "good government" may be attributed to its employees who staff its various administrative departments and agencies. There is general agreement that no other state has civil servants who are more dedicated or have greater professional competence and that California's merit system is primarily responsible for the high caliber of its civil service.

California's civil service system originated with the Progressives, who in 1913 enacted legislation requiring that many positions be filled by competitive examinations. It was given constitutional status in 1934, when the voters approved an initiative amendment sponsored by the state employees. This amendment provided for a state Personnel Board of five members appointed by the governor for ten-year overlapping terms. The length of terms for board members was intended to curtail the possibility of political influence on the civil service.

The Personnel Board is responsible for recruiting, examining, classifying, and training state employees, and for determining the pay rate of each classification. As in the federal civil service, each position is arranged in a class according to the degree of responsibility it entails and the training and skill required. Within each class, pay is uniform, and state law requires that the pay for each job be comparable to that paid in private business. This provision, together with the lobbying efforts of the California State Employees Association, is largely responsible for the salary increases that have been needed to meet the steadily rising cost of living and to make state employment attractive to well-qualified people.

Approximately 98 percent of all state personnel now work under the jurisdiction of the Personnel Board. Excluded are appointees of the governor—including agency and department heads and their top assistants; members of numerous boards and commissions; employees of the legislature and the courts; and employees of the state colleges and state university, which have their own personnel systems.

State finance

THE PROCESS AND POLITICS OF BUDGETING The governor has the chief responsibility for the preparation of the budget. Working with the Director of Finance and other executive officials, he both plans the state's expenditures and recommends measures to provide the necessary revenue. His role in the budgetary process makes his the greatest voice in determining priorities among state programs and agencies. Through his authority to draw up budget proposals—and his use of the item veto—the governor can do more than any other official to decide which programs are to be expanded and which ones will be curtailed or even eliminated. For example, through such decisions the governor can virtually decide how many miles of highway will be built, what new buildings will be constructed, or whether the state colleges and the university will have funds sufficient to provide needed facilities and faculty. The legislature may, of course, revise budgetary items upward or downward, but seldom are the appropriations voted by the legislature greatly different from those recommended by the governor.

Preparing the budget has come to be virtually a year-round process. It begins anew, however, each spring with the governor's annual

"Is that all you government people talk about? Budgets! ... Inflation! ... Depression! ... Why can't you just spend money and enjoy it like we do?" (Reprinted by permission of Lichty and Field Enterprises)

notice to the departments to prepare estimates of the amounts of money they will need during the fiscal year beginning July 1 of the following year. These estimates, which must be submitted to the Department of Finance by October 1, fall into two main categories: money needed for current operations and proposed outlays for capital improvements. In addition, there is a third category: local assistance. Ideally, proposed expenditures should be subject to annual adjustment by the executive agencies, the governor, and the legislature. However, partly because of the ability of some interest groups, like the "highway lobby," to get certain revenues earmarked for their programs and partly because of the necessity of giving counties and school districts advance notice of how much local assistance they can expect, approximately two-thirds of state expenditures are "frozen" by constitutional provisions or statutes.

The Department of Finance, serving as a budget bureau, reviews departmental estimates and revises them so that the programs of the various agencies conform to the governor's general policies. They are then assembled, along with estimates of revenue from existing and proposed new taxes, into a formal budget which the governor submits to the legislature each year shortly after it convenes in January. The budget for the year 1970–1971 was presented in two main volumes, one entitled *Support and Local Assistance*, running to 1,320 pages, and another labeled *Capital Outlay and Five Year Construction Program*, requiring 314 pages. In addition, there was an 884-page *Supplement* giving detailed information on salaries and wages.

The appropriations committees of each house of the legislature, utilizing a number of subcommittees, conduct detailed examinations of the proposed budget for each department, hearing both departmental views and the testimony of the legislative analyst and his staff. Finally, the budget bill as amended is reported out and recommended for passage. Typically, the senate and assembly versions of the bill differ and must therefore be sent to a conference committee. Enactment of the budget requires a two-thirds vote of the full membership of each house. Although the fiscal year begins on July 1, and the budget should be enacted by then, in both 1969 and 1970 disagreements between Governor Reagan and Republican legislators on the one hand and Democrat legislators on the other delayed enactment until after that date. After final adoption by the legislature, the budget bill goes to the governor who often reduces or vetoes individual items. Figure 6-2 indicates the major classes of state expenditures and sources of revenue for 1970–1971.

In the process of reaching decisions regarding the budget, the governor and the legislators consider many factors and encounter pressures from a variety of individuals and organized groups. As would be expected, groups interested in particular programs usually urge higher appropriations for those programs; at the same time, lobbyists for taxpayer associations, organized business groups, individual corporations, and the more affluent customarily urge more stringent budgets and lower taxes. The success of such groups depends partly on the economic and political backgrounds and predilections of the governor and key legislators and partly on the personal relationships between these officials and the various groups.

RAISING THE NECESSARY REVENUES   California does not have a unified department of revenue, although the creation of such a department has been proposed several times. In addition to the Board of Equalization, which is the state's principal revenue agency and which has been discussed, the state depends for the collection of its revenues on a number of other agencies. The Franchise Tax Board assesses and collects both personal income taxes and bank and corporation taxes. The Department of Motor Vehicles collects automobile registration fees, fees for drivers' licenses, and the 2 percent motor vehicle license tax levied "in lieu" of the former personal property tax on such vehicles. Inheritance and gift taxes are collected by the controller, aided by a staff of appraisers working in cooperation with superior court probate judges.

Two additional agencies collecting significant amounts of revenue are the Horse Racing Board, which supervises pari-mutuel betting and collects the state's share of the amounts wagered, and the Department of Alcoholic Beverage Control, which collects fees for licenses relating to the manufacture and sale of alcoholic beverages. A number of other departments also take in various amounts of money; however, in most cases these payments comprise service charges rather than taxes.

CALIFORNIA'S CHANGING REVENUE PATTERN   In the beginning, the state derived all its revenues from only two sources, the property tax and a poll tax. These two alone met all its needs during the first forty-three years of statehood, but virtually every succeeding decade has witnessed

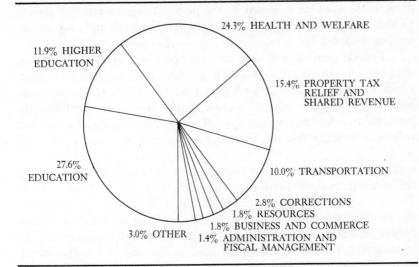

TOTAL EXPENDITURES

24.3% HEALTH AND WELFARE

11.9% HIGHER
EDUCATION

15.4% PROPERTY TAX
RELIEF AND
SHARED REVENUE

27.6%
EDUCATION

10.0% TRANSPORTATION

2.8% CORRECTIONS
1.8% RESOURCES
1.8% BUSINESS AND COMMERCE
3.0% OTHER   1.4% ADMINISTRATION AND
FISCAL MANAGEMENT

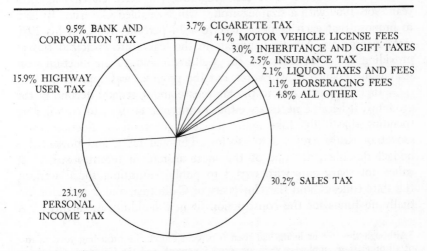

TOTAL REVENUE

9.5% BANK AND
CORPORATION TAX

3.7% CIGARETTE TAX
4.1% MOTOR VEHICLE LICENSE FEES
3.0% INHERITANCE AND GIFT TAXES
2.5% INSURANCE TAX
2.1% LIQUOR TAXES AND FEES
1.1% HORSERACING FEES
4.8% ALL OTHER

15.9% HIGHWAY
USER TAX

30.2% SALES TAX

23.1%
PERSONAL
INCOME TAX

FIGURE 6-2 *Total state expenditures and revenue as proposed by the Governor in 1970–1971 budget*

the imposition of at least one new tax. Today the largest revenue producer is the sales tax followed by the personal income tax, the gas tax (which is more nearly a service charge) and the bank and corporation tax (see Figure 6-2).

Federal grants-in-aid have for years been an important factor in state (and local) finance. Since 1966, California has received more than a billion dollars annually in such payments. Chief among the programs benefiting from such help are welfare, public education, highways, airports, medical facilities, urban renewal, and public housing. Despite the volume of such grants-in-aid, there will undoubtedly be pressure for more.

RECENT DEVELOPMENTS   Even though state taxes and federal grants-in-aid have increased, the problem of raising the necessary revenue is serious. To meet a growing deficit in funds, Governor Reagan in 1967 proposed the largest tax increase in the state's history, totaling nearly a billion dollars. It included raising the sales tax an additional 1 percent and increasing the taxes on personal income, businesses and corporations, cigarettes, and liquor. Due largely to these higher taxes and to substantial cutbacks ordered in several programs, the state ended the fiscal year 1968–1969 with a sizable surplus, which enabled Governor Reagan to propose that each taxpayer receive a 10 percent credit on his 1970 state income tax. Many Democrats in the legislature criticized this as providing larger benefits for the well-to-do and as an election year stratagem designed to win votes, but the proposal was approved.

In 1970, partly due to the tax rebate and a general decline in the economy, it became necessary either to increase taxes or to curtail state spending drastically. Like many previous governors in election years, Governor Reagan refused to ask for additional taxes, and presented a budget described as "one of the most austere in recent history." It called for sharp cuts with regard to public education, social welfare, the state colleges, and the University of California, and it provided virtually no funds for the construction of new buildings or facilities.[7] A

[7] Although the cost of living had risen 6 percent during the preceding year, salaries of all other state employees were increased 5 percent, and the California Coordinating Council for Higher Education had recommended salary increases of at least 7 percent in order to keep California faculty salaries comparable with those in other states, faculty members of the state colleges and the University of California received no increase at all.

tax revision plan sponsored by Governor Reagan—providing for an increase of 1 percent in the sales tax, withholding of state income taxes, and an increase in certain bank and corporation taxes, with the new revenue going to home owners and renters in tax relief—was rejected by the legislature.

Looking to the future, there is no doubt that several changes need to be made regarding California's revenue system. First of all, the federal government should assist the states (1) by taking over most of the burden of social welfare and (2) by sharing with the states a portion of the money collected through the federal income tax. The state government in turn should accept major responsibility for the cost of public education and thus relieve the local communities of excessive dependence upon the property tax. It is also apparent that additional sources of state revenue will be needed. The principal alternatives appear to be (1) increased rates and perhaps lower exemptions on the personal income tax, (2) increased rates for the bank and corporation taxes, (3) increases in the liquor and tobacco taxes, (4) an increase in the tax on horse racing, and (5) a severance tax (that is, a tax on removing from the earth irreplaceable natural resources like oil, natural gas, and minerals of various kinds).[8] Two basic revenue problems will confront California during the years ahead: keeping annual revenues abreast of service requirements and achieving greater equity in the entire tax system.

[8] The other leading petroleum-producing states—Louisiana, Oklahoma, and Texas—all receive a sizable amount of their revenue from severance taxes. Due primarily to the influence of the oil lobby in California, efforts to this date to enact a severance tax have been defeated in the legislature.

CHAPTER 7

LAW AND JUSTICE

The two distinctively political branches of the government, the legislature and the executive, together make the law, often on the basis of recommendations of the governor. Under the separation-of-powers principle, a third branch, the judiciary, is the final authority on the interpretation of the law. Application of the law usually begins with a decision of some state or local administrative officer—such as an inspector, a police officer, or a district attorney—who believes the law requires him to act in a certain way in a given situation. Such a decision may result in a case, which will be tried in court where the decision will be reached as to the manner in which a law is to be enforced.

The administration of justice begins with the people. They have the opportunity to elect honest, responsible legislators to write the laws; they have the obligation to vote directly on the election or retention of judges; and, through the initiative and referendum, they have the means to make or defeat a law themselves. In addition, a few serve on grand juries charged with examining broadly the management of public business and the general observance of criminal statutes, and many more are called for service on trial juries.

THE MACHINERY OF JUSTICE

Executive agencies

Executive agencies play important roles in the interpretation and application of the law. Few laws are self-executing. In practice, therefore, they are no better than their enforcement. The State Department of Justice, operating under the direction of the attorney general, devotes the major share of its energies to the improvement and enforcement of criminal law. Justice depends ultimately upon the courts; but, before a dispute reaches them, and particularly in the case of criminal law, it depends upon the vigilance and impartiality of administrative officials—from the policeman to the attorney general—whose responsibility it is to ensure day-by-day compliance with the law. Unless these public servants are well selected and well paid, unless they know their business and bring resolution, restraint, and dedication to their tasks, the administration of justice falters at the start. For the ordinary citizen, "due process of law" depends largely on the manner in which these officials perform their duties.

California law has gone a long way toward supplementing regular courts with a system of administrative tribunals and of complementing judicial justice with administrative justice. On ordinary tax matters, for example, justice depends for all practical purposes on the Franchise Tax Board or the State Board of Equalization; and justice with respect to utility rates depends upon the Public Utilities Commission. The decisions of agencies like these are reviewable by the courts, but the technical aspects of the issues involved are invariably so much more weighty than the purely legal aspects that the courts have recognized that to ascertain the technical facts is in effect to settle the case.

The bar

The effective administration of the judicial process per se depends upon three major groups of persons—the attorneys, the trial juries, and the judges. The judge on the bench is of first importance in the administration of justice; however, the lawyers who comprise the bar are of nearly equal significance. It is the attorneys, trying to serve their clients, who bring most of the business of litigation into the courts and who make the system of adversary proceedings work. So serving, an attorney at law is legally an officer of the court and is bound by its rules.

California is one of a growing number of states that have state-organized bars. With headquarters in San Francisco, the state bar fixes the qualifications for admission to the practice of law, prescribes and administers the examinations, and formally recommends to the supreme court which candidates should be admitted to practice. (In cases of violation of the profession's code of ethics, it also advises the court on the revocation of licenses.) Attorneys general, district or prosecuting attorneys, city attorneys, and county counsels are members of the bar with special responsibilities. They are the chief law officers of the governments to which they are attached and as such are responsible in court not only for general counsel but also for safeguarding the interests of the people collectively.

Special mention should be made, with regard to criminal justice, of the importance of prosecution and adequate counsel for defendants. Although it was the practice originally for most suits alleging violation of the law to be launched through indictments drawn by grand juries,[1] now the all-but-universal rule is that an accusation is brought in the form of an "information" drafted by a prosecuting attorney. The larger and more progressive counties have in recent years counterbalanced the public prosecutor with a public defender whose task it is to ensure defendants in criminal proceedings their legal rights when they cannot afford to retain a private attorney. As an indication of the importance

[1] A grand jury of nineteen members must be summoned annually by the superior court in each county but its principal function is to investigate the operation of the local governmental offices and to indict officials believed guilty of malfeasance in office. Generally, grand juries are used to bring indictments in criminal cases involving lay citizens only if major crimes are involved.

of this service, the staff of the public defender's office in San Bernardino County carries the burden of the defense in about three-quarters of all felony cases.

Trial juries

Trial juries are selected from panels of prospective jurors prepared by the jury commissioner. Although juries usually consist of twelve persons, if the opposing attorneys agree, a smaller number may be used. The use of juries is far less frequent than is ordinarily supposed. They are never used in suits at equity and are used in suits at civil law only if one of the parties to the case demands it and the amount of damages at stake exceeds $150. They may always be demanded in criminal cases, but today nine out of ten accused prefer the judge alone. Juries are used most frequently in suits over damages for personal injuries.

THE CALIFORNIA JUDICIAL SYSTEM

One of the characteristics of American government is a dual court system. The federal government and the individual states each has a complete system of courts. Although the federal government has exclusive jurisdiction over some kinds of cases, the great majority of cases are tried in state and local courts. State courts are authorized to handle most of the cases that may be tried in federal courts and many other kinds of cases in addition. Hence, the average person is more likely to come into contact with state rather than with federal courts.

California, like most other large states, has four levels of courts: minor courts (justice and municipal courts) of limited jurisdiction; trial courts (superior courts) of general jurisdiction; intermediate appellate courts (district courts of appeal); and its own supreme court (see Figure 7-1).

Municipal and justice courts

At the bottom of the judicial hierarchy are the municipal and justice courts. Each county has at least one municipal or justice court. Munic-

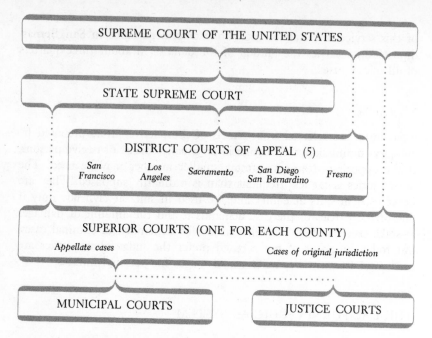

FIGURE 7-1 *Diagram of the California court system*

ipal courts are established in judicial districts of 40,000 or more persons and justice courts in smaller judicial districts. In 1970, there were 75 municipal court districts and 244 justice court districts in the state. Smaller municipal court districts have only one judge, but larger districts may have several. The Los Angeles municipal court district is the largest; it has approximately sixty judges.[2]

Municipal and justice courts have three principal types of jurisdiction. (1) They are authorized to hear minor criminal (misdemeanor) cases, involving such matters as illegal parking and other traffic violations, breaches of the peace, and violations of local ordinances. Their jurisdiction is limited to offenses carrying penalties not exceeding a fine of $1,000 and a year in jail for municipal courts, and a fine of $1,000 and six months in jail for justice courts. Approximately 90 percent of the cases heard by municipal and justice courts involve illegal parking

[2] In 1970 there were a total of 115 municipal county judges in Los Angeles County and 326 in the state.

and other traffic violations. Many of these violations are settled out of court by the defendant simply paying a fine. (2) These courts may hear and dispose of civil cases involving small sums of money. Their jurisdiction extends to civil suits for damages up to $5,000 in municipal courts and up to $500 in justice courts. (3) They may issue warrants for the arrest of persons charged with major crimes (felonies); conduct preliminary examinations into such offenses; and if the evidence is sufficient, bind the suspects over to the superior court for trial. During the fiscal year ending June 30, 1969, a total of more than 11,300,000 cases were filed in municipal and justice courts (see Table 7-1).

Superior courts

Each county has a superior court. These are general trial courts where most of the major civil and criminal cases originate. In the smaller

TABLE 7-1 *Work loads of California's lower courts*

Type	Approximate Number annually
MUNICIPAL COURT FILINGS	
Illegal parking	5,353,601
Other traffic violations	3,636,123
Assorted misdemeanors*	429,053
Preliminary hearings in cases of felony*	101,012
Small claims	277,404
Other civil suits	286,541
Total	10,065,734
JUSTICE COURT FILINGS	
Illegal parking	353,383
Other traffic violations	737,809
Misdemeanors*	79,924
Preliminary hearings in cases of felony*	9,649
Small claims	55,727
Other civil actions	16,236
Total	1,252,728

* Misdemeanors are minor crimes; felonies, major crimes.
SOURCE: Judicial Council, *Annual Report of the Administrative Office of the California Courts for 1968–1969*, San Francisco, 1970, pp. 106, 108.

counties the superior court has only one judge, but among the larger counties the number varies. For example, in 1970 the superior court of Los Angeles County had 134 judges, San Francisco County had 24, and San Diego and Alameda counties each had 22.[3] Each judge in his own courtroom hears cases assigned him. In counties with two or more superior court judges, the judges select one of their members as presiding judge. In the more populous counties, some judges are usually assigned to particular types of cases, such as juvenile, domestic relations, or probate. In the larger counties, there may also be geographic decentralization with individual judges assigned to specific areas.

Superior courts have original jurisdiction over civil suits involving claims of $5,000 or more, and all matters of divorce, probate, or guar-

[3] There were a total of 408 superior court judges in the state in 1970.

Note in this courtroom of the Superior Court of Los Angeles (a) the witness box directly at the left of the judge's bench; (b) the stenographer's desk immediately in front of the bench; (c) the long table in the foreground for the plaintiff, the defendent, and their attorneys; (d) the jury box at the left; and (e) the desk for the other court attachés at the right

dianship. Cases of these types constitute by far the largest proportion of superior court business. The superior courts also have original jurisdiction over all juvenile cases[4] and major criminal cases (under state law) involving sentences of a year or more in prison. Superior courts exercise appellate jurisdiction over cases appealed from municipal and justice courts, but these constitute less than 1 percent of the cases heard in superior courts (see Table 7-2).

District courts of appeal

Although in most states, cases appealed from the trial courts go directly to the state supreme court, California has intermediate appellate courts. These courts have as their basic purpose relieving the state supreme court of some of its appellate burden. Both the nature and the volume of business in the district courts of appeal and the supreme court are

---

[4] The juvenile court is a separate court designed to handle cases of offenders up to eighteen years of age. It is basically a civil court, not a criminal court; the youth is not accused of a crime even though the offense with which he is charged would be a crime if committed by an adult. In practice, the juvenile court, which is based on the philosophy of protection of the child, has tended to deny the young offender certain constitutional rights guaranteed adults. The California Juvenile Court law passed in 1961 and amended in 1967 has given the young offender some rights formerly denied him. He is still given preferential treatment in some ways, but he may not be released on bail pending his trial and he may not have a jury trial.

TABLE 7-2 *California superior courts: filings by type of proceeding*

Divorce, separate maintenance, and annulment	120,740
Probate and guardianship	58,312
Personal injury, death, and property damage	48,967
Civil actions not otherwise classified	87,483
Insanity and other infirmities	20,430
Juvenile	73,612
Criminal	68,159
Appeals from lower courts	3,131
Habeas corpus	3,814
Total	494,011

SOURCE: Judicial Council, *Annual Report of the Administrative Office of the California Courts for Fiscal Year 1968–1969*, San Francisco, February, 1970, p. 90.

vastly different from those in the trial courts below. Fewer cases are heard and the atmosphere is one of calm, unhurried deliberation. No jury is ever used and there is an absence of histrionics. Opposing attorneys present oral arguments, but much of the work is done through the preparation of papers based on the close reading of relevant precedents.

California is divided into five appellate court districts. Three of these districts are further divided into divisions: There are five divisions in the district in which Los Angeles is located, four in the San Francisco district, and two divisions in the San Diego-San Bernardino district. There are three or four judges in each division, making a total of forty-four appellate court judges. Customarily, at least three judges together hear each case. In recent years, approximately 60 percent of all appeals have been criminal cases and the remainder civil suits. These courts also review decisions of the state's quasi-judicial agencies, such as the Public Utilities Commission and the Industrial Accident Commission. California's appellate courts also have some original jurisdiction consisting largely of the issuance of extraordinary writs: habeas corpus (requiring a person being held by law enforcement officials to be brought before a court); mandamus (ordering an inferior court, officer, or corporation to perform some particular act); or a writ of prohibition (forbidding some specific act).

The supreme court

California's highest court is the state supreme court, consisting of a chief justice and six associate justices. The headquarters of the supreme court is in San Francisco but it also holds sessions in Los Angeles and Sacramento. The supreme court has both original and appellate jurisdiction. The former is limited largely to issuing extraordinary writs. Appeals from death penalties go directly from the superior courts to the supreme court. Other cases are normally taken to a district court of appeal before being brought to the supreme court.

Because of the large number of cases appealed to it, the supreme court must use its discretionary power to decide which ones to review. Unless the supreme court accepts the petition of a litigant that his case be reviewed, the decision of the district court is usually final. In most instances, the cases accepted for review involve a major point of law or a matter of widespread importance. The only appeal from the state supreme court is to the United States Supreme Court, and that is only in cases involving the United States Constitution or federal law.

The judicial council

California has a judicial council, which is charged with maintaining a general surveillance over the operation of all of the state's courts. The council now has twenty-one members: the chief justice of the state supreme court who serves as chairman, one associate justice of that court, three justices from the district courts of appeal, five superior court judges, three municipal court judges, two justice court judges, four attorneys, and one member from each house of the legislature. The council issues rules and regulations governing court procedure and also makes recommendations for new legislation relating to the judicial system. The administrative director of the courts, who is appointed by the council, oversees a staff, which conducts continuous studies to determine ways to improve and expedite the work of the courts. The chief justice, as chairman of the council, may equalize the work load of judges by temporarily reassigning judges from courts having relatively light dockets to others where the case load is heavy.

Terms, selection, and removal of judges

Except for a few incumbents on justice courts,[5] all judges must be attorneys who were admitted to the practice of law in California at least five years before their appointment or election. Terms of office for justice, municipal, and superior court judges are six years; for district courts of appeal and supreme court justices, terms are twelve years.

In theory, California has an elective judiciary, with all judges being elected on a nonpartisan ballot (see Figure 7-2). In actual practice, the California judiciary is almost as fully appointive as is the federal bench. The governor is authorized to fill all judicial vacancies (except in justice courts)[6] caused from death, retirement, or the creation of new judge-

[5] Before 1950, justice court judges were not required to be attorneys, but since then each new justice court judge must either be an attorney or pass an examination prescribed by the judicial council.
[6] A vacancy on a justice court between elections is filled by appointment by the board of supervisors in the county.

JUDICIAL

FOR CHIEF JUSTICE OF THE SUPREME COURT

Shall _____ be elected to the Office for the term prescribed by law?	YES	
	NO	

FIGURE 7-2 *Form of ballot for election of justices of the supreme court, justices of the district court of appeal, or judges of the superior court in counties where the voters have given their approval*

ships. Hence, most judges are initially appointed by the governor, who in recent years has appointed an average of seventy to eighty judges a year. Any person selected by the governor as a justice of an appellate court or the supreme court must be approved by the Commission on Judicial Appointments, consisting of the chief justice, the attorney general, and the appropriate senior appellate justice. The approval of this commission is likewise required for appointments to the superior courts in those counties that have adopted this plan.

In order to continue in office, a newly appointed judge must file as a candidate in an election following his appointment and at the expiration of each subsequent term. Appointees typically seek reelection term after term and usually without opposition. Indeed, in the case of a justice of the supreme court or the district courts of appeal the incumbent simply "runs against his record"—he may not be opposed by another candidate. The only question on the ballot is whether he shall be elected to another term.

Actually, the California hybrid appointment-election system for selecting judges has much to commend it. The average voter finds it difficult to decide which of two or more candidates would make the better judge, but from reading newspapers he should be able to determine if a judge has performed his duties in a responsible and competent fashion. Thus, most judges are initially chosen by the governor, who is in a better position than most voters to make this decision; but periodically every person on the bench must submit himself to the electorate to be judged on his actual record.

Until a decade ago, California had no practical method for removing before the expiration of his term a judge who was incompetent or irresponsible. Recall by the electorate and impeachment or censure by the legislature were possible but all proved unduly cumbersome. In 1960, the voters approved a constitutional amendment creating a Commission on Judicial Qualification, which is authorized to request the state supreme court to take action against any judge not properly performing his duties. The commission may receive complaints, conduct hearings, and recommend action to the supreme court. The supreme court may immediately retire a judge suffering from permanent mental or physical disability; and it may remove or censure a judge for misconduct in office, nonperformance of duties, or intemperance. In virtually every instance, however, when investigations by the commission have revealed unfitness or incapacity for judicial offices, the judge under investigation has resigned or retired.

Due process of law

Nothing is more fundamental to the achievement of justice than due process of law. The meaning of this basic concept can perhaps best be explained by noting the successive steps in the trial of a person charged with a major crime. To begin with, there must be a law to which the alleged felony can be related, for an act becomes a crime only when it involves the violation of a specific law. Someone may break the peace, but he can be brought into court only if he breaks it in a way that has been prohibited by law.

There must next be a formal accusation by information or indictment. In the course of this stage, the person involved will normally have been arrested and subjected to preliminary questioning. "Due process" demands that he be promptly informed of the reason for his detention. Should the police fail to explain why they are holding him, he (or a person on his behalf) may ask the court to issue a writ of habeas corpus commanding the police to bring him before the bench to show cause for his detention. Unless proof of the crime is evident or the presumption of guilt is great, he is then entitled to be released on reasonable bail pending trial.

Third, he has a right to counsel of his own choosing; and, if he is without means for retaining an attorney, the court must assign counsel to him. Fourth, "due process" calls for the accused to enter a formal plea in response to the charge made against him (presumed here for purposes of analysis to be "not guilty"). Assuming that the accused and his attorney have decided to request a trial by jury, the next step involves the selection of a jury of his peers.

Next comes the trial proper: the presentation of evidence and counterevidence, examination and cross-examination, argument and counterargument—with the jury deciding points of fact, the judge deciding points of law. The submission of evidence and argument completed, the judge instructs the jury; it retires for deliberation, and subsequently presents its findings on the facts: guilty or not guilty. (If it cannot agree, the judge orders a retrial.) The judge then considers the law, and (assuming a verdict of guilty) pronounces the penalty. Sentencing may occur at once or in due course, but in either case it may entail neither an excessive fine nor cruel or unusual punishment. In the meantime, the defendant always has the right to appeal to a higher court if he believes himself deprived of justice. Finally, assuming the appeal is not granted, the judgment of the court is carried into force.

CORRECTIONS AND CRIME CONTROL

Of the thousands of persons convicted in California every year, only about 4 percent are sent to a state prison or correctional institution. All the others are either placed on probation under the supervision of a probation officer or sentenced to a short term in a local jail or sent to a juvenile hall. The 4 percent who are imprisoned are committed either to the Department of Corrections or to the Youth Authority. These departments have two primary functions: protecting the public by confining the criminal and trying to rehabilitate the criminal.

Treatment of adults

California's *Penal Code* has as one of its distinctive features an Indeterminate Sentence law prescribing minimum and maximum sentence for each crime. Unless the crime is murder, the judge simply sentences the offender for the period provided by the statute. When an adult is committed to a state correctional institution, he is first sent to a reception-guidance center (at Chino or Vacaville), where he undergoes extensive diagnosis to determine what factors caused his criminal behavior and the most effective means of countering them. The guidance center staff then recommends placement in the correctional institution best suited to the inmate's needs. After a convicted person has served six months, the Adult Authority reviews his case and determines his sentence. The legislature has given the Adult Authority considerable latitude with regard to fixing the length of a sentence; for instance, a person convicted of forgery may be imprisoned for any term ranging from six months to fourteen years. Theoretically, a criminal may be paroled after serving for as little as one-third of a minimum statutory sentence, but in virtually every instance an inmate serves considerably longer than the minimum time before being paroled. Of these imprisoned, 98 percent return to society on parole or discharge.

The Department of Corrections' custodial and training facilities now include some twelve institutions for men, one for women, and in addition forty conservation camps. Approximately 45 percent of the inmates require no more than minimal custody; 53 percent fall in the medium classification; only 2 percent need to be held under maximum security. California's correctional program includes academic and vocational training; group counseling and group psychotherapy; individual counseling and psychiatric services; industrial training; and a wide variety of recreational activities.

Treatment of juveniles

California follows the well-established principle that juvenile delinquents should be separated from hardened criminals. It is the responsibility of the Youth Authority to rehabilitate young offenders and to cooperate with local communities in the prevention of juvenile delinquency. During the 1960s, juvenile arrests increased substantially, largely due to the rapid increase in the illegal use of drugs. In 1968 (the most recent year for which data are available), there were 42 percent more arrests among persons under eighteen than in 1960, a total of 366,451 juvenile arrests. Of those arrested, the great majority were released, locally detained, or placed on probation. However, 4,689 were committed to state institutions. The Youth Authority, headed by a board of six appointed by the governor, is responsible both for those committed to state institutions and for those released on parole. For the purpose of diagnosis, treatment, and custody, it operates two reception center–guidance clinics, six vocational schools, and three camps.

The Youth Authority has undertaken two experimental programs designed to improve the effectiveness of delinquency prevention and rehabilitation. The first, the Community Treatment Project established in 1961, was instituted to provide intensive treatment and supervision for juvenile delinquents in their home communities as an alternative to the more traditional institutionalization and parole. The second experimental program consists of the Youth Service Bureaus which have been established in nine counties since 1968. The principal purpose of these bureaus is to coordinate delinquency prevention programs and to provide direct services for youths, including recreational opportunities and employment counseling.

PROBLEMS AND SUGGESTED REFORMS

Through the combination of generally enlightened legislation, impartial judges, and lawyers of high professional and ethical standards, California has gone far toward ensuring a reliable system of justice. Many imperfections remain, however, and it is important to note at least the more significant among them.

Congestion and delay

Justice delayed, runs an old saying, is justice denied. A few years ago, a joint legislative committee found that because of procrastination, compounded in a number of cases by short hours and long vacations, some superior court judges, mainly in rural areas, were taking "up to two years and more" to dispose of some of their civil cases. As for the courts in the larger urban centers, they often have clogged calendars and huge case backlogs, too; but, with the help of the judicial council, they have made progress both in reducing the number of cases awaiting trial and in speeding up proceedings once the trial begins. The key factors in this improvement have been (1) better *calendar management*, (2) greater use of pretrial and settlement conferences, (3) more effective assignment of judges and more extensive use of retired jurists, and (4) the readiness of the legislature to create additional judgeships to handle the ever-mounting volume of litigation as the population of the state increases.

Reduction of costs

One of the most serious impediments to justice is its cost. A citizen may have certain rights under the law, but they lose their meaning if he is unable, because of the expense involved, to go into court and sue for them. There can be little doubt that uneasiness over prospective costs deters many people from either going to court at all or persisting in their suits through all possible stages of appeal. The situation is one calling for a variety of remedies. Many courts could clearly do more to speed up their processes and thus save money as well as time for litigants. In civil cases, persons of limited means could often make greater use of the legal aid bureaus commonly supported by lawyers as a philanthropic service; and the public defender is available to assist the poor person. Those having disputes involving small amounts of money (up to $300) can avail themselves of the services of the small claims court where the use of lawyers is not permitted.

There is a need for new approaches. Many years ago, the cost of justice in the case of claims arising from industrial accidents and illnesses became so great that the legislature devised a special agency and process to handle them. Every progressive state now has a quasi-judicial commission to handle such claims under a program of workmen's compensation insurance. Former Governor Brown once suggested applying this system also in the field of claims for damages arising out of automobile accidents. The legislature has done no more than study the problem; but because of the tremendous cost of justice in many auto injury cases, it should give serious attention to the establishment of an administrative tribunal for handling such cases.

The death penalty

California remains one of the states that impose capital punishment, yet this policy is being questioned by an increasing number of citizens each year. The evidence that fear of execution serves as a deterrent is uncertain or questionable at best; and, for the criminal whose financial resources enable him to appeal his case without limit, the chances of his having to pay the supreme penalty are very small. However, the legislature has been opposed to abolition of the death penalty.

Greater regard for civil rights

Civil rights has become a watchword in this country. It is now one of the prime concerns of courts and law enforcement officials everywhere. Through decisions of the United States Supreme Court, the rights of persons accused of crimes have been extended or more rigorously protected, and the state and local governments have been held to higher standards of "equal justice under law" with respect to the selection of juries, housing, and educational and employment opportunities. Now is the time for greater creative efforts on the part of all branches and units of government, for segregation, discrimination, and denial of basic civil rights are still all too real. Working for their elimination is one of the challenges of the 1970s.

CHAPTER 8

LOCAL GOVERNMENT

Although the federal Constitution recognizes only two levels of government—national and state—there is a third level, local government, which is as vital, indispensable, and firmly established as the others. One of the distinguishing features of the American political system is the vigor and independence of local communities. The overall local government pattern has been the creation of one type of general-purpose unit for rural areas, the county; and another for urban communities, the city or municipality. In addition, most states have also found it necessary to establish special-purpose units of several varieties. Among these, school districts are the most numerous, but some half dozen other types are also quite important.

It is part of the folklore of the American people that democracy begins at home—in the neighborhood, the small community, and the city. Democracy is an experiment in its local setting quite as much as in the national, and it is a mistake to assume that what happens on the local scene is democratic just because it occurs at the "grass roots." The politics of local government cannot be made democratic by definition. Governments of cities, counties, schools, and special districts, like those of states or nations, are democratic only if they are democratic in practice. Civic apathy on the part of some, plus a readiness to exploit the public on the part of others, occasionally make a mockery of democracy on the local level. For popular government to succeed, it is necessary that the political process be visible and understandable to the voters, and that the press and public give serious attention to local affairs.

California's pattern of local government is not a result of a logically designed system but of a process that has developed to meet changing needs. A general outline of local government in California is shown in Table 8-1.

COUNTY GOVERNMENT

Under the constitution of 1849 the legislature was empowered to establish a system of county government, and one of the first measures it enacted created twenty-seven counties. Some of the counties, especially in the then sparsely settled south, were enormous in size, reflecting the earlier pattern of local government under Mexico and Spain. As the state grew in population, the legislature carved additional counties out

TABLE 8-1 *California's pattern of local government*

Counties (including city-county of San Francisco)	58
Cities (as of 1970)	410
School districts (as of 1968)	1,100
Special districts other than school districts (51 types)	3,811
Total number of local governmental units (approximate)	5,379

As is explained in the text, the figures for cities, school districts, and special districts vary, often from month to month.

of the original group until by 1907 all fifty-eight had been established, most of them by special acts.[1]

In 1910, the legislature set the minimal population figure for new counties at 10,000 and the minimal area at 1,200 square miles, providing at the same time that no county could be divided if the effect would be to reduce its population below 20,000. It did not, however, combine small counties formed earlier so that they would conform to this standard. Although the ideal was a system of reasonably uniform counties, there is more variety in size and population in the counties of this state than in any other. The prize anomalies are, of course, the contrasts between Alpine, with about five hundred persons, and Los Angeles, with more than 7 million; and between San Francisco with 42 square miles and San Bernardino with 20,175 (see Figure 8-1).

Historical background

From 1850 to 1911, every county, with one exception, employed the same form of government because they all operated under a general law. The exception was San Francisco, which became a consolidated city-county in 1856 when San Mateo County was formed from its southern "half." In 1911, with the adoption by constitutional amendment of the principle of *county home rule*, counties were granted much the same freedom of choice with respect to the form of their government that had been accorded to cities several decades earlier. To date, ten counties have availed themselves of the privilege of writing their own charters under this amendment.[2] The present pattern consists of forty-seven standard, or general-law, counties, ten charter counties, and the consolidated city-county of San Francisco (which also has a home-rule charter.)

[1] Initially many counties and cities were created, each by a separate statute. Since such special legislation often involved favoritism, the constitution was changed to provide that no local units may be established or incorporated except by general law. Today all counties and cities must be organized as the "general law" pertaining to them stipulates unless, by taking advantage of constitutional "home rule," they draft and adopt a charter calling for a different kind of organization.

[2] The counties are: Los Angeles, 1912; San Bernardino, 1912; Butte, 1916; Tehama, 1916; Alameda, 1926; Fresno, 1933; Sacramento, 1933; San Diego, 1933; San Mateo, 1933; and Santa Clara, 1950.

FIGURE 8-1 *The counties of California*

GENERAL-LAW COUNTIES County government cannot be explained by the familiar legislative-executive-judicial separation of powers so basic in national and state government. County courts are really parts of the state judicial system; there is no independent, elective chief executive corresponding to the President or governor; the boards of supervisors exercise executive as well as legislative powers; and the voters must choose officials for several essentially administrative positions as well as general policy-making representatives.

As may be seen from Figure 8-2, under the general-law form of county government, voters are confronted by a long nonpartisan ballot, which includes candidates for numerous minor as well as several major offices. Such a ballot handicaps the making of public policy and the administration of public services in several ways. (1) The average voter cannot readily inform himself on pertinent qualifications of all candidates. (2) The failure to distinguish between those offices that involve policy making (and should be elective) and those that are administrative (and should be appointive) makes it difficult to ensure that administrative positions are filled with professionally competent persons. (3) The resulting fragmentation of authority means that it is impossible to get the benefits of coordinated management or unified responsibility.

Whatever success counties have achieved under the general law is due partly to the good judgment and cooperative spirit of the elective officers themselves; partly to the coordination achieved by the supervisors through budgetary control or through the device of an administrative officer; and partly in the plan of the legislature permitting offices to combine in eight different ways, such as assessor and tax collector, or clerk, auditor, and recorder.

HOME-RULE OR CHARTER COUNTIES According to the constitution, any county may undertake the drafting of a home-rule charter by simply electing a board of fifteen so-called *freeholders* whose duty it is to draw up within six months a proposed charter. After publication of the charter ten times in a daily newspaper of general circulation, the document must, within sixty days, be submitted to the qualified voters of the county. If approved by a majority, it must be submitted to the legislature, where its acceptance can normally be taken for granted.

Most counties that have drafted charters for their own government have achieved two basic improvements: (1) they have shortened their ballots by making several previously elective offices appointive,[3] and

---

[3] All county officials except the supervisors are potentially subject to appointment, but even Los Angeles County continues to choose its sheriff, assessor, and district attorney by popular election (see Figure 8-3).

The voters, by direct election, choose the following officers, all of whom have four-year terms and are elected simultaneously with the Governor, but on a non-partisan basis.

DISTRICT ATTORNEY	BOARD OF SUPERVISORS	TAX AND LICENSE COLLECTOR
SHERIFF		CORONER AND/OR PUBLIC ADMINISTRATOR
CLERK	5 in all counties except San Francisco which has 11.	SUPERINTENDENT OF SCHOOLS
AUDITOR-CONTROLLER		
TREASURER	Terms are staggered in all cases, half being elected every 2 years. Vacancies are filled by appointment of the Governor.	BOARD OF EDUCATION
RECORDER		SUPERIOR COURT JUDGE(S)
ASSESSOR		MUNICIPAL AND JUSTICE COURT JUDGE(S)

(APPOINTED BY THE SUPERVISORS)

Health Officer
Welfare Director
*Medical Director
Agricultural Commissioner and Livestock Inspector
Farm Adviser
Road Commissioner and/or
*Public Works Director
  Surveyor or Engineer
*Fish and Game Warden
Sealer of Weights and Measures

*Administrative Officer
*Civil Service Commission
*Retirement Commission
  Planning Commission
*Planning Director
*Purchasing Agent
*County Counsel
*Librarian
*Board of Trade
*Board of Public Welfare

*Public Defender
*Building Inspector
*Civil Defense Director
*Fire Warden
*Law Librarian
*Veterans Service Officer
*Airport Manager
*Air Pollution Control Officer
*Recreation Director
*Registrar of Voters

*Indicates optional office

OTHER OFFICERS, BOARDS, AND COMMISSIONS

Probation Officer: usually appointed by Judge of the Juvenile Court on nomination of Probation Committee.
Probation Committee: 7 members appointed by Judge of Juvenile Court.
Parole Board: composed of Sheriff, Probation Officer, and 1 member appointed by the Superior Court.
Board of Law Library Trustees: 3 Superior Judges, 1 Municipal Judge (if there are any), and 2 other members, normally someone from the Bar Association and a member of the Board of Supervisors.
Board of Election Commissioners: Board of Supervisors serves ex officio.
Board of Equalization (in re tax assessments): Board of Supervisors serves ex officio.
Boundary Commission: composed of Assessor, Auditor, Surveyor, Planning Director, and Chairman of Board of Supervisors.
Grand Jury: Composed of 19 citizens selected by the presiding Judge of the Superior Court.

FIGURE 8-2   General-law or standard form of county government

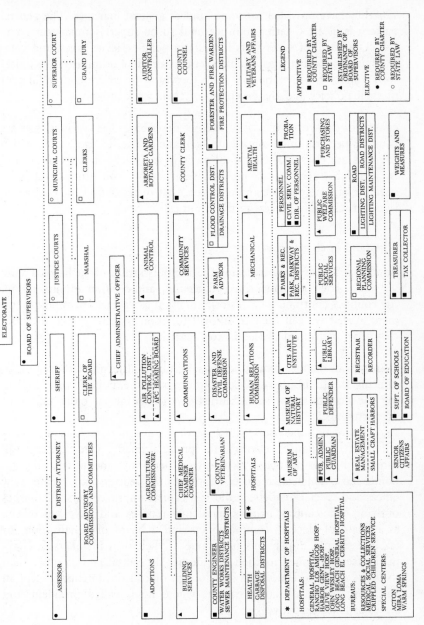

FIGURE 8-3 *Organization of Los Angeles county government*

(2) they have provided for some kind of general manager. The general pattern is clear: Charter counties tend to be supervisor-manager counties. The board of supervisors formulates policies, levies taxes, and votes the budget; the manager, chief executive, or chief administrative officer works under the direction of the supervisors to ensure the fulfillment of their policies and the execution of their work programs.

CLASSIFICATION OF COUNTIES Before describing the various services counties perform, mention should be made of the strange way in which counties are classified. Classification is based solely on population and is carried to such an extreme that each county constitutes a class by itself. It has one purpose and only one, that of regulating the compensation of the various officers in the counties.

Functions of county government

Besides acting as local units for the administration of such basic state services as law enforcement, record keeping, and election administration, the counties continue their historic function as agencies of rural government. What we call their traditional functions consist of the activities they have performed in these two capacities.

TRADITIONAL OFFICES AND FUNCTIONS Probably the simplest way of indicating the traditional services county governments perform is by listing the powers and responsibilities of their principal older offices or "departments."

Board of supervisors, which serves as a county legislature, enacts all county ordinances, oversees all county property, votes all expenditures, and levies all taxes. It supervises personnel and purchasing, appoints most nonelective officers, approves the master plan, creates new offices and special districts, authorizes capital improvements, establishes outlying civic centers, reviews grand jury reports, and serves, ex officio, as a board of election commissioners and a board of equalization for tax assessments. Supervisors name one of their own members as chairman, often in annual rotation, but he has no special powers other than to preside at board meetings and to sign official documents (except in San Bernardino, a charter county, where he is called president and serves as chief executive).

District attorney, who prosecutes all persons accused of crime and, in the absence of a separate county counsel, advises the county on legal matters and represents it in court.

Sheriff, who keeps the peace, operates the jail, regulates traffic, assists in rehabilitating delinquents, and cooperates with federal and municipal officials in riot and demonstration control and in the apprehension of drug law violators.

Clerk, who serves as chief record keeper for the board of supervisors and the superior and lower courts and, in the absence of a separate registrar of voters, as chief elections officer.

Superintendent of schools, who, with advice from the board of education, supervises the operation of local school districts to ensure compliance with the *Education Code* and actually manages the affairs of smaller districts when they default on their responsibilities.

Grand jury, which investigates the functioning of county government for the purpose of discovering whether there has been official misconduct. It hears evidence against persons suspected of crime but not formally charged and decides whether they should be indicted and brought to trial.

Other traditional county officials include the treasurer, recorder, assessor, tax and license collector, auditor-controller, and coroner. Their functions are generally indicated by their titles.

CHANGING CHARACTER OF SOME CALIFORNIA COUNTIES During the past half century, and especially during the last generation, California's tremendous growth has so greatly "urbanized" many counties that the old distinction between peopled cities and "barren" county territory has been evaporating, especially around every sizable municipality.

Although residents of unincorporated settlements around cities are often motivated by a desire for cheap land and the avoidance of city taxes, they find that they need many municipal-type services. When this happens, they may, instead of asking for annexation or forming a regular city government of their own, take one of several other alternatives. (1) They may turn to the county for help (which leads inevitably to the criticism that they are asking for city services without being willing to pay for them). (2) They may form an independent special district with its own governing board to provide the services desired or, as an alternative, ask the board of supervisors to form and run some kind of service district for them. (3) Under the Lakewood Plan, originally developed in the Los Angeles area in the 1950s, they may incorporate and contract with the county for needed services. (Already-existing cities may do the same.) The result of all these developments is that every county that experiences any significant population growth has to supplement its old-line functions with a wide assortment of new ones involving what would formerly have been regarded as city services.

NEWER OFFICES AND FUNCTIONS Urbanization and other social developments have thus necessitated the addition of new county officials and functions to the traditional ones listed above. The following departments or offices tend to reflect the more recent socioeconomic problems and population growth.

County manager, executive, or administrator, who is appointed by the board of supervisors and serves at its pleasure. Regardless of his title, it is his function to advise the board on matters of policy and to ensure the efficient administration of whatever decisions the supervisors make. Approximately three-quarters of the counties have such officers.

Civil service or personnel commission, which administers the classification, recruitment, examination, compensation, promotion, grievance, vacation, sick leave, and retirement programs for county employees in classified positions.

Planning commission, which conducts studies of physical, economic, and social resources and of residential and industrial problems; prepares plans for the board of supervisors, showing how best to ensure orderly physical development; and, upon adoption of a master plan and zoning ordinance, enforces zoning standards.

Health officer, who safeguards and promotes public health through environmental sanitation, communicable disease control, and public health nursing services.

Medical or hospital director, who supervises county hospitals and medical and hospital service for the indigent; he also provides care for the mentally ill before their commitment to a state hospital.

Welfare director, who administers general relief for the poor and categorical public assistance programs for needy children, needy aged, and the blind; supervises child adoption; licenses foster homes for children and boarding homes for the aged. In some counties, he is advised by a board of public welfare.

Road commissioners and/or directors of public works, who design and supervise construction and maintenance of roads and bridges. They administer the affairs of lighting and sanitation districts for which supervisors serve as the governing board.

Public defender, who provides legal counsel to accused persons financially unable to retain attorneys for their protection.

Probation officer, who provides probation service to superior, municipal, and justice courts and has responsibility for juveniles needing shelter or ordered to be detained.

Among the other newer officials are the county counsel, agricultural commissioner and livestock inspector, farm adviser, sealer of weights and measures, fish and game warden, librarian, building inspector, fire warden, civil disaster or defense director, veterans service officer, and air pollution control officer. Once again, their functions are indicated by their titles.

MUNICIPALITIES

No institution built by man is more paradoxical than the city. It creates splendor, but it also breeds slums. It reveals man's concern for his fellowmen, but it likewise brings out the worst in human nature. It is clear that the civic and social problems involved in the wholesale urbanization of American life pose for American democracy some of the toughest issues it has ever had to face. As Governor Edmund G. "Pat" Brown once said: "Until recent years, Americans were free to push west and build new cities when the old became too crowded or too blighted. But California is the last frontier. It is here or nowhere, now or never, that men will stand up to the challenge of the city."

The life style of approximately 90 percent of California's people depends primarily on the economic opportunities, cultural amenities, and public services provided by cities. All of these in turn depend on the adequacy of municipal government and its capacity for responding to changing social needs.

City and state

Before describing the forms of municipal government, some explanation should be given of legal and working relations between city and state. All local units are legally creatures of the state, but cities rank above other subdivisions as units of genuine self-government, (1) because they ask to be created and (2) because they are general-purpose in character. It is nevertheless an established principle in municipal law (called Dillon's rule) that cities have no inherent power and that every argument with the state relative to their authority must be resolved against them. While this creates difficulties for the modern municipality, the handicaps faced by California cities tend to be minimal. This is due to the facts that any city over 3,500 in population may write its own charter if it wishes and that the *Government Code* takes a broad view of municipal functions and grants municipal power accordingly.

California was one of the first states to adopt home rule, allowing cities to frame their own charters. Today, however, the classification of cities into general-law and home-rule (or charter) categories has little significance, because by general law California grants all cities a greater range of authority than many other states allow their municipalities under home rule. California cities are free, for example, to change their form of government by ordinance; of the communities adopting the council-manager or council-administrator plan, three times as many have done so by this method than have used the charter-drafting process.

In their dealings with the state, municipal governments can usually count on the sympathetic interest and support of their senators and assemblymen, but they also have a powerful common spokesman in the League of California Cities, which is probably the strongest such league in the country. It is particularly helpful in matters of law and finance and should be even more effective in serving the cities now that the legislature has been reapportioned on the basis of "one man, one vote." Some metropolitan centers—for example, Los Angeles and San Francisco—also maintain high-caliber lobbyists in Sacramento when the legislature is in session.

Forms of city government

Books on state and local government ordinarily speak of four standard forms of municipal government: (1) weak mayor-council, (2) strong mayor-council, (3) commission, and (4) council-manager. Municipal government in California, however, does not conform to this pattern. Nearly all of the smaller cities, amounting to roughly half of the state's 400 cities, govern themselves by the mayor-council plan outlined in the general law, while a few cities have adopted modifications of it under home rule. Most of the remainder use either the council-manager form or a variant type known as the *council-administrator*, or CAO (chief administrative officer) form. A few cities, like Los Angeles and San Francisco, have forms of government that are *sui generis* (unique). Since Fresno's abandonment of the commission form in 1957, no city in the state uses that plan.

Figures 8-4, 8-5, and 8-6 illustrate the principal forms of city government by outlining the organizations of three representative cities that use them.

MAYOR-COUNCIL SYSTEMS California's general law vests responsibility for handling a city's business in a five-member elective council, the four-year terms of two members overlapping those of the other three. In the weak mayor-council form of government, the mayor is chosen by the council from within its own circle, not to act as a chief executive but mainly to serve as presiding officer. Ordinarily, a clerk and a treasurer are also elected, but these offices may be made appointive if the voters approve. The historic pattern has been for the council itself to manage the affairs of the community—writing its ordinances, levying its taxes, adopting its budget, and appointing and dismissing its employees. In most small places where the need for strong policy leadership and for professional management is at a minimum, the weak mayor-council form of government operates quite well.

Where rapid growth, high taxes, or the need for improved services have seemed to indicate the desirability of having clearer lines of responsibility or more professional management, some cities have availed themselves of their privilege under home rule to write a charter providing for the strong mayor-council form with an elected mayor. Others have taken advantage of the leeway permitted by the general law itself and, by ordinance, have adopted the council-manager plan or some variation of it. Because of their size, Los Angeles and San Francisco both need vigorous executive leadership; and their charters, which are separately described below, provide for independently elected mayors

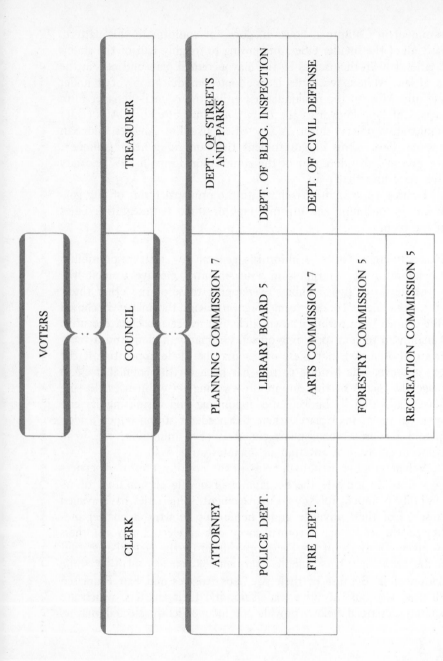

VOTERS

COUNCIL

CLERK

TREASURER

ATTORNEY

POLICE DEPT.

FIRE DEPT.

PLANNING COMMISSION 7

LIBRARY BOARD 5

ARTS COMMISSION 7

FORESTRY COMMISSION 5

RECREATION COMMISSION 5

DEPT. OF STREETS AND PARKS

DEPT. OF BLDG. INSPECTION

DEPT. OF CIVIL DEFENSE

FIGURE 8-4 General-law form of municipal government, illustrated by Carmel-by-the-Sea

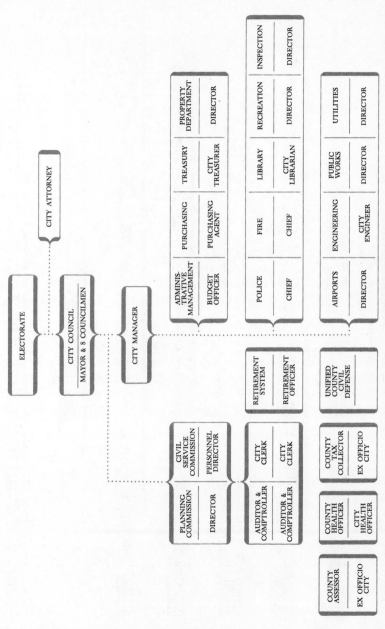

FIGURE 8-5 *Council-manager form of municipal government, illustrated by the city of San Diego, one of the largest in the country using this form*

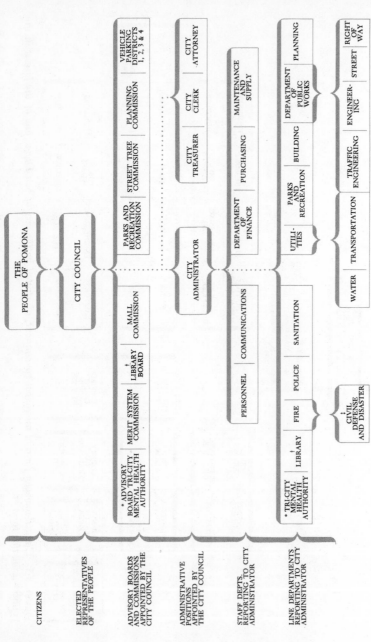

CITIZENS

ELECTED
REPRESENTATIVES
OF THE PEOPLE

ADVISORY BOARDS
AND COMMISSIONS
APPOINTED BY THE
CITY COUNCIL

ADMINISTRATIVE
POSITIONS
APPOINTED BY
THE CITY COUNCIL

STAFF DEPTS.
REPORTING TO CITY
ADMINISTRATOR

LINE DEPARTMENTS
REPORTING TO CITY
ADMINISTRATOR

THE
PEOPLE OF POMONA

CITY COUNCIL

*ADVISORY
BOARD TRI-CITY
MENTAL HEALTH
AUTHORITY

MERIT SYSTEM
COMMISSION

†LIBRARY
BOARD

MALL
COMMISSION

PARKS AND
RECREATION
COMMISSION

STREET TREE
COMMISSION

PLANNING
COMMISSION

VEHICLE
PARKING
DISTRICTS
1, 2, 3 & 4

CITY
ADMINISTRATOR

CITY
TREASURER

CITY
CLERK

CITY
ATTORNEY

PERSONNEL

COMMUNICATIONS

DEPARTMENT
OF
FINANCE

PURCHASING

MAINTENANCE
AND
SUPPLY

†TRI-CITY
MENTAL
AUTHORITY

LIBRARY

FIRE

POLICE

SANITATION

UTILI-
TIES

PARKS
AND
RECREATION

BUILDING

DEPARTMENT
OF
PUBLIC
WORKS

PLANNING

‡CIVIL
DEFENSE
AND DISASTER

WATER

TRANSPORTATION

TRAFFIC
ENGINEERING

ENGINEER-
ING

STREET

RIGHT
OF
WAY

*The Pomona City Council serves as governing body of the authority by joint powers agreement with Claremont and La Verne.
†The library board administers the library subject to certain fiscal, personnel, and purchasing controls exercised by the city council and its appointed officers.
‡Civil defense is attached to the fire dept. for administrative and training purposes but reports to the city administrator under disaster conditions.

FIGURE 8-6 *Council-administrator or CAO form of municipal government, illustrated by the city of Pomona*

having considerable power. Yet a number of medium-sized cities have also written charters establishing the strong mayor-council form or some variant of it.

COUNCIL-MANAGER PLAN   Though there may be variations in detail from city to city, the essential features of the council-manager plan (which was first used in Staunton, Virginia, in 1908) are that the council, a lay body elected by the voters, determines policies, makes all appropriations, levies the taxes, and checks on the general management of municipal affairs but employs a professional executive to serve as the chief administrative officer and to carry out official policies. In the plan's pure form, the manager has indefinite tenure at the pleasure of the council and has the authority, as long as he retains its confidence, to draw up and oversee the execution of the budget; to direct the city's work program; and, most significant of all, to advise the council on matters of policy.

Once policies have been decided and appropriations made by vote of a popularly elected council, there is nothing undemocratic about their being translated into action through efficient administration, particularly when the executive in charge is selected by the council and may at any time be removed by it. Proponents of the council-manager plan claim that it is the formula for making democracy work: combining popular control over policy with efficiency and responsibility in administration. Opponents criticize it on the grounds that it neglects the need for political leadership and that, for the sake of efficiency, it exposes the city to the risk of "dictatorship." Probably the best way to underscore the merits of this modern form of municipal government is to say that for nearly fifty years it has been the basis of the National Municipal League's *Model City Charter*.

COUNCIL–CHIEF ADMINISTRATIVE OFFICER (CAO) FORM   Some cities that have resisted the council-manager plan have instituted a modification of it which for convenience may be called the council-CAO form. The title of the executive officer may be city administrator, administrative officer, or chief administrative officer. The essential difference between this plan and the council-manager plan is that a CAO has a position of less prestige than a manager and also a lesser range of authority with regard to finance and personnel. He tends to be a coordinator rather than a genuine manager. Proponents of this plan believe that it is possible to get good administration without giving any professional executive the authority to appoint and remove heads of departments or to oversee the execution of the budget. Others disagree and argue that the council-CAO plan is a weak imitation of the real thing and it is in no sense more democratic than the council-manager form.

SAN FRANCISCO San Francisco is a consolidated city-county heavily built up over most of its 42 square miles. Its government, headed by an elected mayor who has extensive powers, combines certain features of both the mayor-council and the council-CAO forms, as well as a number of features borrowed from the general-law form of county government. Perhaps the most satisfactory way to describe the plan is by presenting an outline of it (see Figure 8-7).

LOS ANGELES Organized under a long and complex home-rule charter, the city of Los Angeles has a rather unusual form of government, characterized by the extensive use of citizens' commissions which advise and to some extent direct the heads of departments. The mayor has a position of considerable strength and also enjoys the assistance of a CAO, but it is the various lay commissions which make the plan unique (see Figure 8-8). The occasional feuding between Mayor Samuel W. Yorty and the city's fifteen-member council leaves little doubt, however, that charter reform can be postponed only at serious costs to its citizens.

Incorporation of cities

Under California's *Government Code* it is easy to incorporate a city. Any portion of a county not already incorporated and containing as many as 500 inhabitants may become a municipal corporation. The essential steps are as follows:

1. Filing with the board of supervisors a notice of intention to circulate a petition for incorporation, and within ninety days filing with the board a second petition asking the supervisors to call an election on the issue. The second petition must be signed by at least 25 percent of the voters in the area, and these must include the owners of at least 25 percent of the land (according to value) included in the proposed city limits.

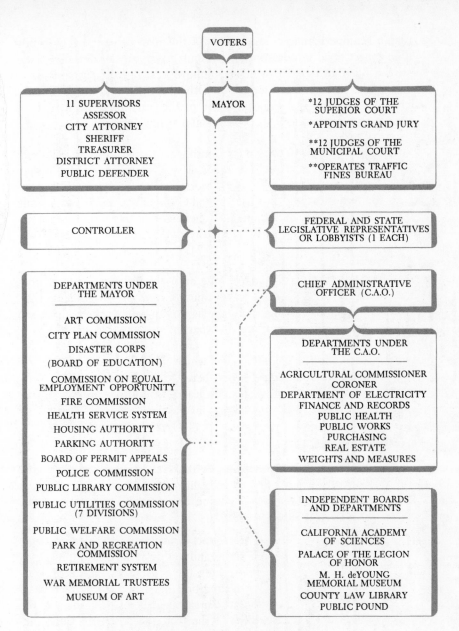

FIGURE 8-7 *Organization of the city-county of San Francisco*

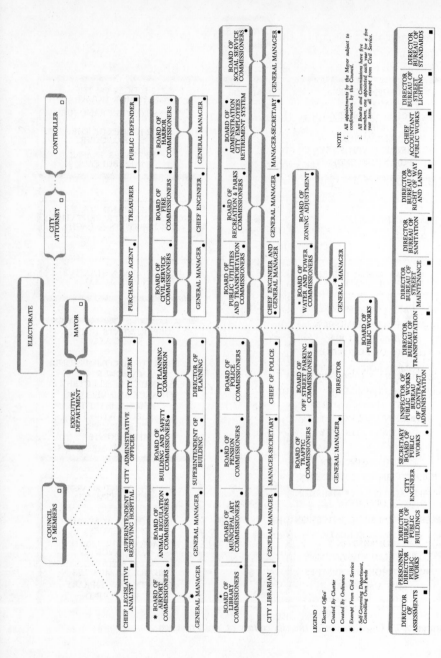

FIGURE 8-8 *Organization of the city of Los Angeles*

ELECTORATE

CONTROLLER □

CITY ATTORNEY □

MAYOR □

COUNCIL 15 MEMBERS □

EXECUTIVE DEPARTMENT ■

CHIEF LEGISLATIVE ANALYST ■

SUPERINTENDENT RECEIVING HOSPITAL ■

CITY ADMINISTRATIVE OFFICER ■

CITY CLERK ●

PURCHASING AGENT ●

TREASURER ●

PUBLIC DEFENDER ■

BOARD OF AIRPORT COMMISSIONERS *●

BOARD OF ANIMAL REGULATION COMMISSIONERS ●

BOARD OF BUILDING AND SAFETY COMMISSIONERS ●

CITY PLANNING COMMISSION ●

BOARD OF CIVIL SERVICE COMMISSIONERS ●

BOARD OF FIRE COMMISSIONERS ●

* BOARD OF HARBOR COMMISSIONERS ●

GENERAL MANAGER ●

GENERAL MANAGER ●

SUPERINTENDENT OF BUILDING ●

DIRECTOR OF PLANNING ●

GENERAL MANAGER ●

CHIEF ENGINEER ●

GENERAL MANAGER ●

BOARD OF LIBRARY COMMISSIONERS *●

BOARD OF MUNICIPAL ART COMMISSIONERS ●

BOARD OF PENSION COMMISSIONERS *●

BOARD OF POLICE COMMISSIONERS ●

BOARD OF PUBLIC UTILITIES AND TRANSPORTATION COMMISSIONERS ●

BOARD OF RECREATION & PARKS COMMISSIONERS ●

* BOARD OF ADMINISTRATION CITY EMPLOYEES RETIREMENT SYSTEM ●

SOCIAL SERVICE COMMISSIONERS ●

CITY LIBRARIAN ●

GENERAL MANAGER ●

MANAGER-SECRETARY ●

CHIEF OF POLICE ●

CHIEF ENGINEER AND GENERAL MANAGER ●

GENERAL MANAGER ●

MANAGER-SECRETARY ●

GENERAL MANAGER ●

BOARD OF TRAFFIC COMMISSIONERS ●

BOARD OF OFF STREET PARKING COMMISSIONERS ●

* BOARD OF WATER AND POWER COMMISSIONERS ●

BOARD OF ZONING ADJUSTMENT ●

GENERAL MANAGER ●

DIRECTOR ■

GENERAL MANAGER *●

BOARD OF PUBLIC WORKS ■

DIRECTOR OF ASSESSMENTS ■

PERSONNEL DIRECTOR OF PUBLIC WORKS ■

DIRECTOR BUREAU OF PUBLIC BUILDINGS ■

CITY ENGINEER ■

SECRETARY BUREAU OF PUBLIC WORKS ■

* INSPECTOR OF PUBLIC WORKS BUREAU OF CONTRACT ADMINISTRATION ■

DIRECTOR BUREAU OF TRANSPORTATION ■

DIRECTOR BUREAU OF SANITATION ■

DIRECTOR BUREAU OF STREET MAINTENANCE ■

DIRECTOR BUREAU OF RIGHT OF WAY AND LAND ■

CHIEF ACCOUNTANT PUBLIC WORKS ■

DIRECTOR BUREAU OF STREET LIGHTING ■

DIRECTOR BUREAU OF STANDARDS ■

LEGEND
□ Elective Office
● Created By Charter
■ Created By Ordinance
■ Exempt From Civil Service
* Self-Governing Department, Controlling Own Funds

NOTE
1. All appointments by the Mayor subject to confirmation by the Council.
2. All Boards and Commissions have five members, one appointed each year for a five year term, all exempt from Civil Service.

184

2. Submission of a map of the proposed city to the county boundary commission.
3. Fixing by the board of supervisors of a date for a general hearing on the petition, and hearings on the petition by the board. (Written protests by the owners of 51 percent of the property as measured by assessed value nullify the proceedings.)
4. Designation by the board, with at least two weeks' notice, of a date for an election, followed in due course by the election itself.
5. If a majority votes for incorporation, declaration by the board of the establishment of a new city. If the effort fails, no further move may be initiated for two years.

GENUINE VERSUS ARTIFICIAL CITIES Because of the simplicity of these requirements and the enormous postwar population sprawl, California has experienced a rash of incorporations in recent years. Most of these have been bona fide ventures in the building of new cities, but some appear to have been prompted less by a desire to create the machinery for providing essential public services than by cold calculation designed either to forestall what might be termed logical annexation to an adjacent city or to take advantage of fortuitous provisions in the *Revenue and Taxation Code*. For example, certain manufacturing areas have been incorporated not because they were natural communities but precisely because, through incorporation, the owners of industrial properties could avoid enclosure within a natural or balanced community embracing the homes of their employees and thus escape paying their share of its tax burden. In similar fashion, various other areas have sought incorporation primarily because the fortuitous location of a shopping center has made it possible to establish another kind of tax refuge—a city enjoying so much revenue from the sales tax and business licenses and from its share of the state gas tax and motor vehicle license fees as greatly to lessen if not to eliminate any need for a property tax.

The very shape of some cities generates suspicion as to why they were incorporated. Probably the most flagrant example of a noncity in southern California is the city of Industry which "sprawls across the map of San Gabriel Valley like an underfed dragon" (see Figure 8-9). Sixteen miles long but no more than a stone's throw in width at its narrowest section, it is, because of its factories, the richest city in the valley in terms of assessed valuation of property per capita. It has a

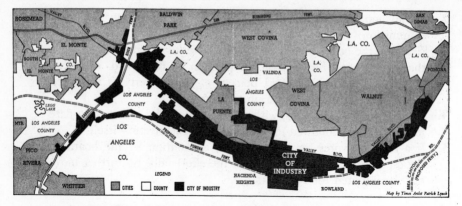

FIGURE 8-9 *City of Industry, Los Angeles County (Patrick Lynch,* Los Angeles Times, *June 26, 1966)*

daytime population of more than 25,000; but, fifteen minutes after the quitting whistle blows, fewer than 800 permanent residents remain.

THE LAKEWOOD PLAN Reinforcing the temptation to incorporate, especially in southern California, has been the introduction of the Lakewood Plan. This is an arrangement that draws its name from the city of Lakewood, near Long Beach, and its practice of buying municipal services from Los Angeles County instead of providing them itself. The plan's feasibility depends entirely on the capacity of the county in which the proposed city is located to "sell" urban services under contract. Once a municipal corporation is formed, all that is required for it to begin functioning as a city is the election of a council, the appointment of an attorney, clerk, treasurer, and preferably a planning commission and manager, and then the negotiation of the necessary contracts.

The Los Angeles supervisors now have the plan reduced to the equivalent of a cafeteria line with a special officer assigned to represent them in the negotiations involved and subsequently to oversee the observance of contracts. The plan has not yet spread extensively to other counties, but the possibility is present. From the angle of municipal self-reliance it would seem to be seriously defective; yet from a larger perspective, it may be for the best. The problem of coordinating the services of local governments in metropolitan areas is so baffling that perhaps a plan involving maximum reliance upon the county deserves encouragement. In any event, the availability of the Lakewood Plan has been a catalytic agent in producing the incorporation fever of the past decade in southern California.

METROPOLITANITIS

The classic concept of a city in America is that of a sizable number of people living in a compact, built-up area serving their local needs through a municipal corporation which they themselves control and support, and surrounded by more or less open country. During the nineteenth century the cities of California matched this model fairly well, but the twentieth century has brought marked changes.[4]

California's fourteen metropolitan areas

The U.S. Census Bureau, mindful of the increasing concentration of population in great cities, has developed the concept of a "standard metropolitan statistical area." This is defined as a county or two or more adjacent counties containing at least one city of 50,000. California now has fourteen such metropolitan areas: Los Angeles–Long Beach, San Francisco–Oakland, San Diego, Sacramento, San Jose, Stockton, Fresno, Bakersfield, Santa Barbara, San Bernardino–Riverside–Ontario, Anaheim–Santa Ana–Garden Grove, Oxnard–Ventura, Salinas–Monterey, and Vallejo–Napa.

BALKANIZATION The term "balkanization," used to describe the fragmentation of an area into small competing factions, is appropriate in describing the situation in urban areas of California. While every one of California's fourteen metropolitan areas in beset by the problem of balkanization, the situation is undoubtedly at its worst in the San Francisco Bay Area and in Los Angeles County. Several years ago a *San Francisco Chronicle* editorial stated: "The simple and sorry fact is that the Bay area is a balkanized area, split by parochialism and petty jealousies

[4] For a more thorough analysis of metropolitan areas and their problems see Henry A. Turner, *American Democracy: State and Local Government*, 2d. ed., New York: Harper & Row, Publishers, Incorporated, 1970, pp. 119–138.

that are serious and costly impediments to sane and efficient development of what is essentially a single metropolitan area." A breakdown of governmental units in Los Angeles County reveals the extent of the problem in that area. In Los Angeles County alone, the work of handling the public business is divided among 487 different local governmental units: 1 county, 77 cities, 67 school districts, and 342 special districts.

Solutions to metropolitan problems

From the positive angle there are a number of things that can be done to ease the evils of metropolitanitis, although all are not equally applicable in every area.

LAFCO   The legislature has authorized each county to set up a Local Agency Formation Commission. Composed of two supervisors, two city councilmen, and a representative of the general public selected by these four, this commission (usually labeled LAFCO) is responsible for reviewing and advising on all applications for the formation of new municipalities or special districts and for annexations to existing units. In addition, it has authority to make recommendations regarding "secessions" from cities as well as proposed changes in the composition of special districts. This procedure promises to deter the incorporation of new local units when their creation would be ill advised.

ANNEXATION OR CONSOLIDATION   Historically, the commonest solution for the problem of proliferation was for the larger of two cities "growing together" to annex the smaller one or, if they were roughly equal in size, for the two to be consolidated. Legally, these options are still open, but in recent years there has been little inclination to use them.

URBANIZING THE COUNTY   As mentioned earlier, in those instances where the whole, or nearly the whole, of a metropolitan area lies within the boundaries of a single county, one of the simplest arrangements for handling areawide functions on a rational basis would be to capitalize on the county for this purpose. Some steps have been taken in this direction in Los Angeles, San Diego, and several other of the larger counties; but much more could be done.

INTERGOVERNMENTAL COOPERATION Voluntary intercounty, intercity, inter-school-district, or, better yet, general intergovernmental cooperation among all local units in a metropolitan area constitutes another potentially fruitful approach to the problem. This is particularly true insofar as regional planning is concerned. Currently, two big experiments of this kind are under way. Both are based on the Joint Exercise of Powers Act which was adopted by the legislature for the express purpose of encouraging such cooperation. One is called ABAG (Association of Bay Area Governments) and the other, SCAG (Southern California Association of Governments).

METROPOLITAN SERVICE DISTRICTS Still another formula is that of service districts, which may be either of the single-service or, preferably, the multiservice type. The Los Angeles and San Diego areas have benefited enormously during the past forty years from the huge Metropolitan Water District of Southern California. In the vital field of mass transportation, two new giants are preparing to serve their respective communities: BART (Bay Area Rapid Transit), in the San Francisco area; and RTD, the Southern California Rapid Transit District, in the Greater Los Angeles area. In the future, emphasis should be on multiservice districts lest the areas be plagued by further fragmentation.

STATE ASSISTANCE Most of the responsibility for improving metropolitan government rests with the people of the given area. Yet the state also has an important role. The legislature should design and make available to civic leaders and political units in metropolitan areas governmental devices of a kind that will encourage and facilitate their adoption. It should also formulate its revenue and expenditure policies in such a way as to offer tangible inducements to local units in a given area to create such a system. Finally, the state should lead in organizing a continuing forum for examining the problems of its cities.

SCHOOL DISTRICTS

California has followed the general American pattern of providing public education through local school districts. Indeed, the pattern of a separate organization for public education is so widely understood and generally accepted that by common consent the term "special districts" is seldom applied to school districts. Public education constitutes such an important and expensive part of local government that it would be desirable to have maximum cooperation between school districts and city and county government. Unfortunately, the possibilities for such cooperation remain largely unexplored.

Four types of districts

School districts comprise the most expensive unit of local government, yet because their responsibility is limited to a single prime function, their basic organization is easily described. Operating under the general supervision of the state Board of Education and Department of Education are four different types of districts: elementary school, high school, unified districts (providing both elementary and secondary education), and junior college. With a few exceptions, each district elects a five-member board of trustees (for four-year terms), and they in turn select a local superintendent who serves as their executive officer and administrative head of the school system.

Elementary districts are naturally the most numerous, but they are steadily being joined with high school districts in their areas to form unified districts. Whatever may have been the need or justification for separate elementary and high school districts originally, there is almost none today. One way in which the state can encourage the merger of elementary districts with the high school districts that the majority of their pupils subsequently attend is to make state aid dependent upon such mergers.

Unification of school districts means merging elementary districts with a high school district in the same area. Consolidation has meant the joining of smaller districts to form larger ones. For many years, educators and public officials urged consolidation because they claimed the larger districts would be more efficient, would provide a broader and more equitable tax base, and would ensure more nearly equal opportunities for students. Now the problems of large school districts are so great that a reevaluation of this concept is taking place.

The Los Angeles school district, which opened its first school in 1855, grew in 115 years to be the nation's largest (in area) urban school district. In 1970, a study made for the state legislature concluded that this huge district epitomized the weaknesses of mass education, noting that it was deficient in providing quality education, failed to accord adequate representation to residents, was lacking in cost efficiency, could not readily be held accountable for its performance, and had not achieved racial integration. In order to provide a means to correct these and other shortcomings, it proposed that the Los Angeles school district be divided into from twelve to twenty-four subdistricts, each with a locally elected board. This plan for decentralization—which envisioned subdistricts remaining in the city school system for purposes of taxing, centralized purchasing, personnel, and routine budgetary services—made a sharp break with the past. This plan, or some similar alternative, may become a model for the decentralization of other large urban school districts.

Decentralization offers no assurance of quality education or improved pupil performance, and per pupil cost may be higher. Neither does it bring integrated schools nearer to a reality. It does, however, put responsibility, decision making, and accountability on a level nearer the people being served. If in this way the schools can be made more responsive to the needs of individuals and communities, solutions to other problems may be more easily found.

SPECIAL DISTRICTS

State law proscribes the powers and functions of cities and counties in such a way that they are unable to cope effectively with problems not coterminous with their boundaries. Adaptability to changing needs for governmental services has been made possible through the creation of special districts that are established under state law for the purpose of providing some limited, and often single, service usually not available from any city or county government. Of the four main types of local governmental units in California, special districts are the most numerous; and they are increasing at a rapid rate. During the decade before 1969, special districts in the state grew by nearly a thousand to 3,811 (see Table 8-2).

One may well ask why there is such a growth of limited-purpose districts. In some instances, a city or county may decide not to undertake some activity because only a limited number of people or only the

Type of district	Number of districts	Type of district	Number of districts
Fire protection	465	Memorial	26
County service areas	377	Water agency and authority	23
Highway lighting	374	Water conservatoin	17
County maintenance	352	Library	14
Cemetery	257	Air pollution control	14
County water	209	Harbors and ports	13
Soil conservation	164	Flood control maintenance areas	13
Community service	162	Community redevelopment and	
Reclamation	154	housing	13
California water	151	Garbage disposal	12
County sanitation	138	Joint highway	10
Sanitary	126	Pest abatement	10
Recreation and park	111	Police protection	8
County waterworks	94	Water storage	8
Hospital	68	Citrus pest control	7
Public utility	66	Transit	7
Municipal water	50	Municipal improvement	6
Mosquito abatement	50	Road maintenance	5
Sewer and sewer maintenance	39	Airport	3
Flood control and water		Bridge and highway	1
conservation	35	Health	1
Joint exercise of powers	35	Parking	1
Storm water drainage and		Sanitation and flood control	1
maintenance	32	Separation of grade	1
Drainage	28	Metropolitan water	1
Permanent road divisions	27	Water replenishment	1
Levee	26	Water conservation	1
		Total	3,811

Roughly two-thirds of these districts have separate boards; one-third are run by county boards of supervisors. A few flood control districts are operated by the state Department of Water Resources.

SOURCE: California State Controller, *Financial Transactions Concerning Special Districts for 1968–1969*, Sacramento: State Printing Office, 1969, p. vii. A separate report is issued on irrigation districts; they are not included in this table.

people in one region have wanted it. The people desiring the service may form a special district. On the other hand, many special districts have been established to provide a common service for the people in several cities and even counties. Other districts have been formed as a means of bypassing legal limits on a city's or county's taxing or borrowing authority.

From the standpoint of control, special districts fall into two classes: (1) those having their own separately elected boards of directors and (2) those for which the county supervisors exercise such power. Even so, the statutes pertaining to these districts are so numerous (some 175 different authorizations), so scattered, and, in many cases, so obscure and unclear, that the official report of the state controller concerning special districts sometimes disagrees with the report published by the county for the same year.

Formerly, most special districts were found in rural areas where they were created to provide such services as fire protection, water supply, soil conservation, or mosquito abatement. However, the larger and more important ones have been established to build and maintain hospitals, parks and recreation facilities, airports, water systems, public power plants, and other kinds of facilities. Although the boundaries of most districts are within or coterminous with those of cities and counties, some such districts overlap both city and county boundaries. The varieties and types of services provided by special districts are shown according to major functional categories in Table 8-2.

Overall record of special districts

A general evaluation of special districts should consider their efficiency, their cost, and their effect on voters. Obviously, with nearly 4,000 such districts, there would be varying rates of efficiency, and some would pay their costs while others would not. As to their impact on the voting public, the sheer numbers of special districts would tend to induce confusion or apathy.

Clearly, it would be a mistake to go on forming special districts at the rate typical of recent years—particularly those districts authorized to perform only a single function. Adherence to five main principles could, however, lead to a simpler, more workable, and ultimately less expensive pattern: (1) consolidation of existing districts wherever compatibility of purposes and minimal boundary adjustments make that a rational possibility; (2) emphasis on multipurpose rather than single-purpose units (public utility districts are already authorized to perform fifteen different functions; community service areas, eleven); (3) utilization of the county supervisors as a governing board unless the district promises to be so important in the lives of its residents that they can be expected to follow its affairs almost as if it were an incorporated community; (4) differential taxation based upon the services actually rendered in each county service area and differential charges wherever operation can fairly be placed on a fee-for-service basis; and (5) creation of a state commission or various regional commissions whose approval would be necessary in order for new special districts to be formed.

FINANCING LOCAL GOVERNMENT

County expenditures and revenues

Comparison of the contemporary pattern of county expenditures with that of ten, twenty, or thirty years ago reveals that the most striking development during the past generation has been an enormous increase in expenditures for welfare, medical care, and corrections. This is the principal danger zone from the standpoint of keeping county expenditures within reasonable limits.

The biggest changes regarding county revenues during the past generation have been the notable decline in the proportion of funds supplied by the general property tax and the tremendous increase in grants-in-aid and shared revenues. Property taxes amounted to more than 75 percent of all revenues in 1930 but less than 35 percent in 1968. Grants-in-aid and shared revenues (of the latter, perhaps the sales, gas, and motor vehicle license taxes furnish the best examples) comprised but 11.9 percent of total county income in 1930; they amounted to more than 45 percent in 1968. In the face of a growing conviction that property, especially residential real estate, is now carrying about as heavy a burden as it can bear, the chances are that as additional funds are needed the counties will either demand more in the form of shared revenues or try to raise more money through service charges (see Table 8-3).

Expenditures	Amount	Percent	Revenues	Amount	Percent
General	$ 468.6	14.5	General property		
Public protection	478.1	14.8	tax	$1,189.2	36.4
Roads	233.5	7.2	Sales tax	51.8	1.6
Health and sanitation	109.1	3.4	Franchise tax	5.2	0.2
Public assistance	1,818.4	56.4	Other taxes	15.5	0.5
Education	49.5	1.6	Licenses and permits	17.4	0.5
Recreation	36.1	1.1	Fines, forfeits, penalties	45.3	1.4
Debt service	23.8	0.8	From use of money and		
Public enterprise	6.7	0.2	property	56.9	1.7
			From the state	781.5	23.9
Total	$3,223.8	100.0	From the federal		
			government	698.1	21.3
			Charges for current service	375.2	11.5
			Other revenue	34.1	1.0
			Total	$3,270.2	100.0

SOURCE: State Controller, *Annual Report of Financial Transactions Concerning Counties of California, Fiscal Year 1968–69*, Sacramento: State Printing Office, 1969, pp. ix, x, xiii, xiv.

Municipal expenditures and revenues

Table 8-4 indicates the nature and volume of municipal expenditures and revenues for 1968–1969. The cities of California are responsible for a steadily lengthening list of services. In terms of cost, they rank: (1) utility enterprises such as water and electricity; (2) police and fire protection; (3) streets and bridges, including lighting and storm drainage; and (4) recreation.

During the past forty years California's cities have experienced a great change in the sources of their revenue. In 1930, they had total receipts of 162.2 million dollars, of which 78.2 percent came from the general property tax and only 3.4 percent from grants-in-aid. By 1968, this pattern had changed radically. Property taxes yielded less than 33 percent, while subventions and grants had risen to more than 20 percent, and many cities had developed a number of additional sources of income. Although there is considerable strength and equity in the present municipal revenue program, the financial position of many cities

Expenditures	Amount	Percent	Revenues	Amount	Percent
General government			Taxes		
Departmental	$311.3	15.5	General property	$666.6	32.0
Nondepartmental			Sales	342.2	16.4
Debt service—interest	37.3	1.9	Franchises	18.4	.9
Debt service—principal	75.8	3.8	Other nonproperty tax	79.1	3.8
Retirement	150.0	7.5	Licenses and permits	104.3	5.0
Other	81.0	4.0	Fines and penalties	55.8	2.7
Public safety	560.9	28.0	From use of money		
Public works	477.0	23.8	and property	93.8	4.5
Health	40.9	2.0	From other governmental		
Libraries	51.7	2.6	agencies	420.0	20.1
Parks and recreation	189.0	9.4	Charges for current services	189.1	9.1
Aid to other governmental			Other revenue	114.0	5.5
funds and units					
City-owned enterprises	25.9	1.4	Total	$2,083.3	100.0
Other	2.8	0.1			
Total	$2,003.6	100.0			

SOURCE: State Controller, *Annual Report of Financial Transactions Concerning Cities of California, Fiscal Year 1968–1969*, Sacramento: State Printing Office, 1969, pp. vii, xii, xiii.

could be improved through increased reliance on business licenses and perhaps also the adoption of a local income tax levied by counties and collected by the state with the revenues distributed to the cities or rural areas on the basis of where the income was actually earned.

School district and special district finance

When the average citizen gets the bill for his property tax, he will find that the largest item represents the cost of public education. The explanation lies in the enormous expansion of the American public school system since World War II—an expansion not only in the percentage of children attending school, but also in the proportion of young people continuing through high school, junior college, and increasingly, senior college or university.

School districts are severely limited in their sources of revenue. At present, they have only three main sources of support: (1) property taxes, (2) charges for services, and (3) state aid. Judging by the appeals school trustees and administrators have made to the legislature, local school districts want state government to commit itself to underwriting at least half the cost of operating the public schools. In 1970, the voters of California defeated an initiative measure sponsored by the California Teachers Association and the County Supervisors Association that would have required the state to finance half of the cost of the public schools.

It is difficult to generalize about the problems of special districts because they vary greatly, not only in size and function but with respect to their sources of revenue. The cardinal point regarding their finances is that many of them receive a large proportion of their total income from user and service charges. For the remainder, however, property taxes and grants-in-aid from the state play an important part in supporting their budgets.

BIBLIOGRAPHY

Chapter 1

BEAN, WALTON: *California: An Interpretive History*, New York: McGraw-Hill Book Company, 1968.

California and the Challenge of Growth, 7 reports, Berkeley: University of California Office of Publication, 1965.

CALIFORNIA DEPARTMENT OF WATER RESOURCES: *The California Water Plan*, Sacramento: State Printing Office, 1957.

————: *California State Water Project*, Sacramento: State Printing Office, published annually.

CALIFORNIA ECONOMIC DEVELOPMENT AGENCY: *California Statistical Abstract*, Sacramento: State Printing Office, published annually.

CALIFORNIA STATE DEPARTMENT OF FINANCE: *California's Population,* Sacramento: State Printing Office, 1969.

CASSTEVENS, THOMAS W.: *Politics, Housing and Race Relations: California's Rumford Act and Proposition 14,* Berkeley: University of California Institute of Governmental Studies, 1967.

COHEN, NATHAN (ed.): *The Los Angeles Riots: A Socio-Psychological Study,* New York: Frederick A. Praeger, Inc. 1969.

DASMAN, RAYMOND: *The Destruction of California,* New York: The Macmillan Company, 1965.

LEE, EUGENE C., and WILLS D. HAWLEY: *The Challenge of California,* Boston: Little, Brown and Company, 1970.

MAGA, J. A.: *Air Resources Management in the San Francisco Bay Area,* Berkeley: University of California Institute of Governmental Studies, 1965.

McWILLIAMS, CAREY (ed.): *The California Revolution,* New York: Grossman Publishers, Inc., 1968.

PENALOSA, FERNANDO: "The Changing Mexican-American in Southern California," *Sociology and Social Research,* vol. 51, pp. 405–417, July, 1967.

REAGAN, RONALD: *Economic Report of the Governor 1970,* Sacramento: State Printing Office, 1970.

RECORD, WILSON: *Minority Groups and Intergroup Relations in the San Francisco Bay Area,* Berkeley: University of California Institute of Governmental Studies, 1963.

RUSTIN, BAYARD: "The Watts 'Manifesto' and the McCone Report," *Commentary,* vol. 41, pp. 29–35, March, 1966.

STEAD, FRANK M.: "How to Get Rid of Smog," *Cry California,* vol. 2, pp. 35–39, Winter, 1966–1967.

WOOD, SAMUEL E., and ALFRED E. HELLER: *California, Going, Going . . . ,* Sacramento: California Tomorrow, 1962.

Chapter 2

Book of the States, Chicago: Council of State Governments, published biennially.

Briefs on a Long Constitution, San Francisco: League of Women Voters of California, 1964.

BUSTERUD, JOHN A.: "Politics of Constitutional Revision," in Eugene P. Dvorin and Arthur J. Misner (eds.), *California Politics and Policies,* Reading, Mass.: Addison-Wesley Publishing Company, Inc., 1966.

CALIFORNIA ASSEMBLY INTERIM COMMITTEE ON CONSTITUTIONAL AMENDMENTS: *Final Report: Constitutional Revision in California*, Sacramento: State Printing Office, 1967.

CALIFORNIA CONSTITUTION REVISION COMMISSION: *Proposed Revision of the California Constitution*, Sacramento: State Printing Office, 1966.

Constitution of the State of California, Sacramento: State Printing Office, 1969.

ELLISON, WILLIAM H.: *A Self-governing Dominion*, Berkeley: University of California Press, 1950.

ENGLEBERT, ERNEST A., and JOHN G. GUNNELL: *State Constitutional Revision in California*, Los Angeles: University of California Bureau of Governmental Research, 1961.

GREENBERG, DONALD S.: "The Scope of the Initiative and Referendum in California," *California Law Review*, vol. 54, pp. 1717–1748, October, 1966.

MASON, PAUL: "Constitutional History of California," in *Constitution of the State of California and of the United States and Other Documents*, Sacramento: State Printing Office, 1969, pp. 75–104.

MUELLER, JOHN E.: "Voting on the Propositions: Ballot Patterns and Historical Trends in California," *American Political Science Review*, vol. 63, pp. 1197–1212, December, 1969.

SUMNER, BRUCE: "The California Constitution Revision Commission," in *Constitution of the State of California and the United States and Other Documents*, Sacramento: State Printing Office, 1969, pp. 109–120.

SWISHER, CARL B.: *Motivation and Political Technique in the California Constitutional Convention, 1878–1879*, Claremont, Calif.: Pomona College, 1930.

VIEG, JOHN A.: "A New Design for California Politics," *Western Political Quarterly*, vol. 13, pp. 692–701, September, 1960.

WOLFINGER, RAYMOND E., and FRED I. GREENSTEIN: "The Repeal of Fair Housing in California: An Analysis of Referendum Voting," *American Political Science Review*," vol. 62, pp. 753–769, Summer, 1968.

Chapter 3

ALEXANDER, HERBERT E., and LAURA L. DENNY: *Regulations of Political Finance*, Berkeley: University of California Institute of Governmental Studies, 1966.

CALIFORNIA ASSEMBLY INTERIM COMMITTEE ON ELECTIONS AND REAPPORTIONMENT: *Report*, Sacramento: State Printing Office, 1961, 1963, 1967.

CALIFORNIA OFFICE OF LEGISLATIVE COUNCIL: *State Elections Code*, Sacramento: State Printing Office, 1963.

CALIFORNIA SECRETARY OF STATE: *Statement of Vote*, Sacramento: State Printing Office, published following every primary, general, or special election.

California Voters Handbook, San Francisco: League of Women Voters, 1970.

CRANSTON, ALAN: "A Million-Dollar Loser Looks at Campaigning," *Fortune*, pp. 124, 278, 289, November, 1964.

GREGG, JAMES E.: "Newspaper Editorial Endorsements and California Elections, 1948–1962," *Journalism Quarterly*, vol. 42, pp. 532–538, Autumn, 1965.

————: *Newspaper Editorial Endorsements: Their Influence on California Politics*. Davis: University of California Institute of Governmental Affairs, 1966.

LANGGUTH, JACK: "Political Fun and Games in California," *The New York Times Magazine*, October 16, 1966.

LEE, EUGENE C.: *California Votes, 1928–1960*, Berkeley: Institute of Governmental Studies, 1963.

LEISTER, D. R.: *California Politics and Problems, 1964–1968: A Selected Bibliography*. Berkeley: University of California Institute of Governmental Studies, 1965.

LEUTHOLD, DAVID A.: *Electioneering in a Democracy: Campaigns for Congress*, New York: John Wiley & Sons, Inc., 1968.

————, with WILLIAM M. REID and WILLIAM MACAULEY, *California Politics and Problems, 1900–1963: A Selected Bibliography*. Berkeley: University of California Institute of Governmental Studies, 1965.

OWENS, JOHN R.: *Money and Politics in California: Democratic Senatorial Primary, 1964*, Princeton, N.J.: Citizens' Research Foundation, 1966.

PITCHELL, ROBERT J.: "The Influence of the Professional Campaign Management Firms in Partisan Elections in California," *Western Political Quarterly*, vol. 11, pp. 278–300, June, 1958.

ROWE, LEONARD C.: *Preprimary Endorsements in California Politics*, Berkeley: Bureau of Public Administration, 1961.

SEABURY, PAUL: "The Antic Politics of California," *Harper's*, vol. 230, pp. 82–93, June, 1965.

WILSON, JAMES Q.: "A Guide to Reagan Country," *Commentary*, vol. 43, pp. 37–45, May, 1967.

WOLFINGER, RAYMOND E., and FRED I. GREENSTEIN, "Comparing Political Regions: The Case of California," *American Political Science Review*, vol. 63, pp. 74–85, March, 1969.

Chapter 4

ANDERSON, TOTTON J.: "California: Enigmatic Eldorado of National Politics," in Frank H. Jones (ed.), *Politics in American West*, Salt Lake City: University of Utah Press, 1969.

———— and EUGENE C. LEE: "The 1966 Election in California," *Western Political Quarterly*, vol. 18, pp. 451–474, June, 1965.

———— and ————: "The 1966 Election in California," *Western Political Quarterly*, vol. 20, pp. 535–554, June, 1967.

BEAN, WALTON: *Boss Ruef's San Francisco*, Berkeley: University of California Press, 1952.

BLAISDELL, DONALD C. (ed.): "Unofficial Government: Pressure Groups and Lobbies," *The Annals of the American Academy of Political and Social Science*, vol. 319, September, 1958.

CALIFORNIA ASSEMBLY INTERIM COMMITTEE ON ELECTIONS AND REAPPORTIONMENT: *Political Party Organization*, Sacramento: State Printing Office, 1963.

DELMATIER, ROYCE D., CLARENCE F. MCINTOSH, and EARL G. WATERS (eds.): *The Rumble of California Politics 1848–1970*, New York: John Wiley & Sons, Inc., 1970.

HARRIS, JOSEPH P.: *California Politics*, 4th ed., San Francisco: Chandler Publishing Company, 1967.

LEE, EUGENE C.: *The Politics of Nonpartisanship*, Berkeley: University of California Press, 1960.

MOWRY, GEORGE E.: *The California Progressive*, Berkeley: University of California Press, 1951.

ROGIN, MICHAEL: "Progressivism and the California Electorate," *The Journal of American History*, vol. 15, pp. 297–314, September, 1968.

WILSON, JAMES Q.: *Amateur Democrat*, Chicago: University of Chicago Press, 1962.

Chapter 5

BEEK, JOSEPH A.: *The California Legislature*, Sacramento: State Printing Office, 1965.

BLAIR, GEORGE S., and HOUSTON I. FLOURNOY: *Legislative Bodies in California*, Belmont, Calif.: Dickenson Publishing Company, Inc., 1967.

BUCHANAN, WILLIAM: *Legislative Partisanship: The Deviant Case of California*, Berkeley: University of California Press, 1963.

CALIFORNIA ASSEMBLY SELECT COMMITTEE ON ASSEMBLY REORGANIZATION: *Report*, Sacramento: State Printing Office, 1969.

CALIFORNIA LEGISLATURE: *Final Calendar of Legislative Business*, Sacramento: State Printing Office, published annually.

————: *Handbook*, Sacramento: State Printing Office, published biennially.

————: *Legislative Advocates and Organizations*, Sacramento: State Printing Office, published periodically.

DOUBLEDAY, D. JAY: *Legislative Review of the Budget in California*, Berkeley: University of California Institute of Governmental Studies, 1969.

DRISCOLL, JAMES D.: *California's Legislature*, Sacramento: State Printing Office, 1969.

GABLE, RICHARD W., and ALEXANDER CLONER: "The California Legislator," in California Constitution Revision Commission, *Proposed Revision of the California Constitution*, Sacramento: State Printing Office, 1966, pp. 145–173.

HINDERAKER, IVAN: "Politics of Reapportionment," in Eugene P. Dvorin and Arthur J. Misner (eds.), *California Politics and Policies*, Reading, Mass.: Addison-Wesley Publishing Company, Inc., 1966.

NATHAN, HARRIET (ed.): *Attitudes, Innovation and Public Policy: A Symposium for the California Legislature*, Berkeley: The University of California Institute of Governmental Studies, 1968.

OHNIMUS, ARTHUR A.: *The Legislature of California*, Sacramento: State Printing Office, 1966.

PRICE, CHARLES M., and CHARLES G. BELL: "Socializing California Freshmen Assemblymen: The Role of Individuals and Legislative Sub-Groups," *Western Political Science Quarterly*, vol. 23, pp. 166–179, March, 1970.

ROBECK, BRUCE: "Impact of Reapportionment on the California Senate," unpublished doctoral thesis, University of California, Santa Barbara, 1968.

Chapter 6

BELL, JAMES R.: *Coordinating California's Governmental Programs*, Berkeley: Bureau of Public Administration, 1959.

———— and THOMAS J. ASHLEY: *Executives in California Government*, Belmont, Calif., Dickenson Publishing Company, Inc., 1967.

BREAK, GEORGE F.: *Agenda for Local Tax Reform*, Berkeley: University of California Institute of Governmental Studies, 1970.

CALIFORNIA ASSEMBLY INTERIM COMMITTEE ON REVENUE AND TAXATION: *A Program of Tax Reform for California,* Sacramento: State Printing Office, 1965.

California Blue Book, Sacramento: State Printing Office, published quadrennially.

CALIFORNIA GOVERNOR: *Budget Submitted to the Legislature,* Sacramento: State Printing Office, published annually.

————: *Reorganization of the Executive Branch of California State Government: Reorganization Plan No. 1 of 1968,* Sacramento: State Printing Office, 1968.

CALIFORNIA LEGISLATIVE ANALYST: *Analysis of the Budget Bill,* Sacramento: State Printing Office, published annually.

CALIFORNIA SENATE FACT FINDING COMMITTEE ON REVENUE AND TAXATION: *Report* (9 parts), Sacramento: State Printing Office, 1965.

CALIFORNIA SENATE INTERIM COMMITTEE ON GOVERNMENTAL ORGANIZATION: *Organization of the Executive Branch of the State Government,* Sacramento: State Printing Office, 1968.

CALIFORNIA STATE DEPARTMENT OF GENERAL SERVICES: *Organization of the Executive Branch of California State Government,* Sacramento: State Printing Office, 1965.

COMMISSION ON CALIFORNIA STATE GOVERNMENT ORGANIZATION AND ECONOMY: *Findings and Recommendations Concerning Reorganization of the Executive Branch of California State Government,* Sacramento: State Printing Office, 1963.

GOVE, SAMUEL K.: "Why Strong Governors?" *National Civic Review,* vol. 53, March, 1964.

HACKETT, BRUCE M.: *Higher Civil Servants in California: A Social and Political Portrait,* Davis: University of California Institute of Governmental Affairs, 1967.

RANSOME, COLEMAN B., JR. (ed.): "The American Governor in the 1970's, *Public Administration Review,* vol. 30, January-February, 1970.

ROSTVOLD, GERHARD N.: *Financing California Government,* Belmont, Calif.: Dickenson Publishing Company, Inc., 1967.

Chapter 7

BADER, HELMUT: "California's Pioneering Courts," in John P. Carney and William M. Alexander (eds.), *California and United States Governments: Readings and Documents,* Boston: Allyn and Bacon, Inc., 1967.

CALIFORNIA ASSEMBLY COMMITTEE ON CRIMINAL PROCEDURE: *Report,* Sacramento: California Legislature, 1963.

CALIFORNIA ASSEMBLY COMMITTEE ON JUDICIARY: *Final Report,* Sacramento: California Legislature, 1963. Also *Report on Problems of the Death Penalty and Its Administration in California,* Sacramento: California Legislature, 1957.

CALIFORNIA JOINT LEGISLATIVE JUDICIARY COMMITTEE: *Report on Administration of Justice,* Sacramento: California Legislature, 1959.

CALIFORNIA JUDICIAL COUNCIL: *Annual Report of the Administrative Office of the California Courts,* Sacramento: State Printing Office, published annually.

CALIFORNIA LEGISLATIVE ANALYST: *Analysis of the Budget Bill,* Sacramento: State Printing Office, published annually.

COOK, BEVERLY BLAIR: *The Judicial Process in California,* Belmont, Calif.: Dickenson Publishing Company, Inc., 1967.

LOS ANGELES COUNTY: *Biennial Report of the Superior Court,* Los Angeles: published in even-numbered years.

ROBINSON, J. EDWARD: *History of the Supreme Court Judges of California,* San Francisco: Bender-Moss Company, 1963.

Chapter 8

ADVISORY COMMISSION ON INTERGOVERNMENTAL RELATIONS: *Annual and Special Reports,* Washington, D.C.: U.S. Government Printing Office, 1966.

BOLLENS, JOHN C., and H. J. SCHMANDT: *The Metropolis,* New York: Harper & Row, Publishers, Incorporated, 1965.

CALIFORNIA ASSEMBLY INTERIM COMMITTEE ON MUNICIPAL AND COUNTY GOVERNMENT: *Multipurpose Districts,* Sacramento: State Printing Office, 1963.

California County Fact Book, Sacramento: California County Supervisors Association, published annually.

CALIFORNIA LEGISLATURE, ASSEMBLY INTERIM COMMITTEE ON REVENUE AND TAXATION: *Report of a Major Tax Study,* 12 parts, Sacramento: State Printing Office, 1964, 1965.

CALIFORNIA SECRETARY OF STATE: *Roster of Federal, State, County, and City Officials,* Sacramento: State Printing Office, published annually.

CALIFORNIA STATE CONTROLLER: *Financial Transactions Concerning Cities,* Sacramento: State Printing Office, published annually.

————: *Financial Transactions Concerning Counties*, Sacramento: State Printing Office, published annually.

————: *Financial Transactions Concerning School Districts*, Sacramento: State Printing Office, published annually.

————: *Financial Transactions Concerning Special Districts*, Sacramento: State Printing Office, published annually.

CARNEY, FRANCIS M.: "The Decentralized Politics of Los Angeles," *Annuals of the American Academy of Political and Social Sciences*, vol. 353, pp. 107–121, May, 1964.

CHAPMAN, JOHN L.: *Incredible Los Angeles*, New York: Harper & Row, Publishers, Incorporated, 1967.

CROUCH, WINSTON W., and Beatrice Dinerman: *Southern California Metropolis*, Los Angeles: University of California Press, 1963.

JONES, VICTOR: "Metropolitan Detente: Is It Politically and Constitutionally Possible?" *The George Washington Law Review*, vol. 35, pp. 741–757, May, 1968.

KENT, T. J., JR.: *Open Space for the San Francisco Bay Area: Organizing to Guide Metropolitan Growth*, Berkeley: University of California Institute of Governmental Studies, 1970.

NATHAN, HARRIET, and STANLEY SCOTT (eds.): *Toward a Bay Area Regional Organization*, Berkeley: University of California Institute of Governmental Studies, 1969.

SCOTT, STANLEY (ed.): *Local Government in a Changing World*, Berkeley: University of California Institute of Governmental Studies, 1970.

SOUTHERN CALIFORNIA RESEARCH COUNCIL: *Taxation by Local Government: A Case Study of Los Angeles County*, Claremont, Calif.: Pomona College Department of Economics, 1966.

TURNER, HENRY A.: *American Democracy: State and Local Government*, New York: Harper & Row, Publishers, Incorporated, 1970.

VIEG, JOHN A. (ed.): *California Local Finance*, Stanford, Calif.: Stanford University Press, 1960.

WARREN, ROBERT O.: *Government in Metropolitan Regions: A Reappraisal of Fractionated Political Organization*, Davis: University of California Institute of Governmental Affairs, 1966.

WOODS, S. E., and A. F. HELLER: *California's Phantom Cities*, Sacramento: California Tomorrow, 1963.

INDEX

207

6417